The Adventures of Another Pooh

The Adventures Of Another Pooh

Caving Explorations and Escapades

David Yeandle

Writers Club Press

San Jose New York Lincoln Shanghai

The Adventures Of Another Pooh
Caving Explorations and Escapades

Writers Club Press
an imprint of iUniverse, Inc.

For information address:
iUniverse, Inc.
5220 S. 16th St., Suite 200
Lincoln, NE 68512
www.iuniverse.com

ISBN: 0-595-22466-0

Printed in the United States of America

To my parents, Frank and Dorothy Yeandle

Some days really don't run according to plan.
—David Yeandle

Contents

Foreword

I've been a caver for more than thirty years. I was lucky enough to start my caving in England during a very exciting period. In the late 1960s and early '70s there was a renaissance in cave exploration in Northern England. Many miles of previously unknown underground passages were explored. I was fortunate enough to be involved in some of these explorations.

Being the first person to enter a new cave is a marvellous thing to do and it is my hope that this book will convey something of the experience of original exploration. That was not my main reason for writing about my adventures though. Being a caver is great fun mainly because of the people that are attracted to this rather odd and sometimes hilarious activity. For me it's the excellent people I have had the pleasure to go caving with that have made my explorations worthwhile. The pages that follow are my attempt to pay tribute to my friends in the caving world.

Pictures and additional stories can be found on my website at **http://www.poohcaving.co.uk/**

David Yeandle

Acknowledgements

I would like to thank the following people for allowing me to use their material: Dave Brook, Lindsay Dodd, Stuart Herbage, Roy Holmes and Pete (Snab) MacNab

Thanks are also due to Tony Jarratt for checking my manuscript and to Charles Muller for the final editing and production.

I also need to thank all the cavers who have helped me out over the years; by doing things like giving me lifts, buying me beer, giving me food, letting me sleep on their floors, lending me equipment and generally putting up with some fairly silly events.

David Yeandle

1

Langcliffe Pot

I could hear a skylark singing high above the moor. I stopped walking and gazed around the sky trying to spot the bird singing this lovely song. It was one of those summer days when the Yorkshire Dales is the best place to be in the whole world. The sun shone in a near cloudless sky and a gentle breeze sent ripples through the meadow grass in the fields below me. The River Wharfe wound its way lazily through the valley bottom and dry-stone walls soared improbably up the steep hillsides into the fells above. I was glad to be in this beautiful place; but soon I would be leaving it all, for the harsh underground world of Langcliffe Pot.

"Come on Pooh," called Dave Brook as he walked on up the hill. "No time for day dreaming!"

As usual, I was at the back of the group. I started walking as fast as I could, fearful that I would be left behind and not be able to find the entrance.

As I carried on up the hill the view across Wharfedale became even more glorious as bleak moorland, hidden becks and distant tops came into view above the fertile valley. To me Wharfedale seemed deeper and grander than the Dales in the Ingleton area. Perhaps this was my youthful imagination, spurred on by the knowledge that Langcliffe was potentially deeper than any of the caves over in the 'classic' areas. I felt both excited and apprehensive at the prospect of this trip. We were planning to dig at the end of the cave and both Dave Brook and Iain Gasson thought the chances of a breakthrough good.

Somewhere under Wharfedale, there must surely be 'The Black Keld Master Cave' and perhaps Langcliffe was going to be the way in. I was very happy to be going on a 'pushing trip' with these legendary cavers. I wanted to prove my worth on their team. This was, I felt, a chance at the 'big time.'

From ULSA Review 8, July 1971, Gasson's Series.
by Dave Yeandle.

In 1968 the ULSA Exploration of Langcliffe was stopped by the onset of bad weather. In the summer of 1970 the club was able to continue its work in this splendid cave. Those present on the return trip were Dave Brook, Iain Gasson, Dave Johnstone, Tony White and Dave Yeandle.

The entrance pitch was quickly descended and the party made its way through the Craven Crawl (210m) and Stagger Passage (610m) to Hammerdale Dub. The party split here; Tony and Dave J making their way up the inlet to finish off surveying and exploration of the Thunder Pot Inlet beyond High Cross, while the remaining three dashed off towards Boireau Falls Chamber and the boulder choke they proposed to examine.

Immediately beyond the Kilnsey Boulder Crawl, D.B disappeared down a hole and proceeded to explore the upstream path of the main stream. Meanwhile Iain and Dave Y pressed on downstream; they were new to the cave and for them it was full of interest. Even so it seemed endless. Soon after their arrival in Boireau Falls Chamber D.B caught them up and announced that he had been able to penetrate upstream parallel to the boulder crawl for about 150m.

The three cavers began work in the terminal boulder choke. Several short digs seemed unpromising but even so the workers had no time to be bored; Iain became stuck when a boulder slipped and he was freed by D.B and Trusty (the crowbar). Retribution was nigh, however, since D.B received a nasty cut hand when another boulder fell on it. More ferreting about was done, when suddenly Iain was onto something. A hole, seemingly leading in the wrong direction, had given access to a cavity in the boulders, and in the floor a small gap enabled him to reach stream level for the first time. By then negotiating feet first, an evil looking slot in the stream course, he was able to enter a larger continuation. To his amazement a sizeable passage developed beyond; the stream ran over a potholed floor. Almost immediately Iain found himself in a chamber at the head of a pitch. He retraced his steps and called for the others to follow through, which they did with difficulty, so devious was the route through the choke. Eventually all three were standing at the head of the pitch—and what a pitch! The passage simply plunged into the depths and the cavers were in fact on a mass of boulders jammed precariously across the top. In the absence of ladders the party busied itself in preparation for the next stage of the exploration. A few of the more dangerous boulders were eased away from the lip, but attempts failed to discover an easier exit to the extension via a mud slope, which ascended from the top of the pitch to boulders which obviously comprised the floor of Boireau Falls Chamber. Presently the explorers cast a last longing look down the pitch and started back to the .surface.

Thrutching sideways out through the Craven Crawl I was tired and cold. But I was doing okay!—not being left behind as on previous trips with these top cavers. I was proud to be a member of the U.L.S.A. I was actually caving with Dave Brook on a major exploration! I was very pleased with myself, and I felt I'd come a long way in my three years of caving.

It had begun with a schoolboy trip to Burrington Combe, in Somerset. We were young lads wanting adventure. Two or three of the boys had been caving before, but it was my first time. As I slithered through the muddy tubes of Goatchurch Cavern and Sidcot Swallet, I thought that maybe I was going to be doing a lot of this thing called caving. It was as though something beyond my control wanted to draw me inwards, away from the mundane world outside, around the next corner, or through the next squeeze just to see what was there. But another part of me didn't want to do these new and frightening things in this strange world of total darkness and horrid mud. This part of me wanted to turn around and hurry back out to the sunshine. I kept following my friends though and when I was back home in Bristol I was elated that I had overcome my fear and kept going. I knew that now I had an exciting new world to explore.

My friend Russell Mines was a member of the Axbridge Caving Group and I joined too. Soon I was travelling over the Mendips with Stuart (Mac) McManus and Tony Jarratt on motorcycles of dubious legality and questionable mechanical soundness. (Mac was rumoured to run his on paraffin!) We drank scrumpy cider and fell over a lot; which I suppose was a silly way to spend my paper-round money.

One Monday night in the Axbridge Hut, Mac and I were without money and we wanted food and cider. We were the only cavers left over from the weekend and we knew there was money in the little envelopes in the hut fees box. I can't remember which one of us finally suggested that we borrow some hut fee money; anyway we rigged up a fishing device out of wire and a stick and soon became rich beyond measure! We did write an I.O.U on a piece of paper and posted it into the box. The club committee were unimpressed with us despite our owning up.

With Russell, Mac, Tony, and other Axbridge members, I did trips to most of the major Mendip caves. By now caving was the main thing in my life and I was getting ambitious. I wanted to go to Swindon's 12, and to the bottom of the Berger; and I wanted to go caving with my hero—Mike Boon.

I had heard that the Bristol Exploration Club (BEC) constituted the local Mendip hard men and I decided to join them to further my caving career. I had no idea how I was going to do this, though actually it happened very quickly. My arrival at the Belfry was not auspicious. I was dumped at the door, tied up and drunk, late at night by Mac, Tony Jarratt, and other Axbridge members. It seems they got fed up with me always going on about joining the BEC and agreed that it was indeed a good idea. Some say I was tied up in barbed wire and minus my trousers. I don't remember this myself, and anyway Mac and Tony would not have been so mean! Another version of the story is that I was in fact tied to the milk churns at the end of the Belfry turn off. I think this may have been on another occasion though! I don't think the BEC liked me very much at first and some of them wouldn't talk to me. They let me make them tea in the Belfry though and soon kind people like Alan Thomas, Chris (Zot) Harvey, Colin Priddle, John Riley, Dave Irwin and Roy Bennett were taking me caving. I became the Belfry Boy.

THE BELFRY BOY
Sung to the tune of Sweet Lorraine
by Pete MacNab

Well, I'm the Belfry Boy,
I'm every other bugger's favourite toy,
Oh how it always seems to give them joy,
To put me in bloody pain.

Oh how they treat me hard,
Kick me all around the Belfry yard,
Lord, you ought to see how I am scarred,
From when they shoved me up the drain.

And when a member calls,
I dash inside so they can black my balls,
And splatter me around the Belfry walls,
Till I've nearly gone insane.

They sit me in a chair,
Rub jam and marmalade into my hair,
I sit and smile as if I couldn't care,
But later hang my head in shame.

And then they all insist,
That I am something called a masochist,
Especially when they all come back pissed,
And want to play their silly games.

But now I sit and wait,
Because I'm glad to know that some day fate,

Will bring along a brand new inmate,
And then I'll kick the Belfry Boy.

Alan Thomas had been on expeditions to Greece with Jim Eyre where they had bottomed The Abyss of Provatina. These were the days of using ladders for big pitches and Alan ran BEC trips to Yorkshire where the objectives were usually pots with deep entrance pitches. I was very excited when Alan agreed to take me on one of his northern trips. I was piled into the back of his car along with 'Buster' the dog and large tins of Spam left over from an expedition.

Camping at Skirwith Farm, we did Alum Pot, Marble Steps, and Long Kin West. I was very impressed with this Yorkshire potholing but my ladder climbing was abysmal and it took me more than half an hour to be dragged up the 91m daylight pitch of Long Kin West. Consequently I was banned from attempting the main shaft of Gaping Gill on ladders, which was the main objective of the visit. I was very disappointed but managed to get to Main Chamber via Bar Pot. I was awestruck by the huge dimensions of the main chamber with the water from the beck above crashing down onto the boulders on the floor. The daylight filtering down the main shaft gave the whole place an eerie atmosphere. It was all very exciting and I decided I wanted to live in Yorkshire and do a lot of this sort of caving.

Back on the Mendips in the Hunters' Lodge Inn, I started to hear stories about the incredible revival of exploration in the Dales. The relatively recent innovation of the wetsuit had enabled northern cavers to push the frontiers forward and Dave and Alan Brook were the most successful of a new generation. Miles of new cave had been opened up by this legendary pair and members of the University of Leeds Speleological Society (U.L.S.A). I had already decided that an academic career would best serve my caving ambitions and once I heard about ULSA my choice of University was an easy one. This did mean that I had to actually start to do some schoolwork in order to get good A levels. Zot had no faith in my plan! "You're as thick as pig shit! How can you go to University?" He had a point! I had narrowly avoided being kicked out of the sixth form for exam results worse than 10%. I did start to work though, and even stopped caving for a few weeks prior to my A Levels. To everybody's surprise, and my parents' delight, I got into Leeds on a Physics Honours course.

Exams over, I settled down to a summer of caving in Austria and the Mendips with my BEC friends. The Austrian trip was to the Ahnenschacht, lead and organised by Alan Thomas. We explored several hundred metres of new cave, living mostly on Spam and reconstituted mashed spud. As usual, Alan didn't charge me enough for my share of the petrol.

I managed to combine moving north with a caving weekend. There was a BEC trip to Lancaster Hole so I threw in a few extra clothes and one or two textbooks with my caving gear and got a ride north with Martin Webster. After the trip he dropped me off in Skipton and I travelled to Leeds by bus. The University had arranged lodgings for me and the landlady was rather shocked at my appearance when I turned up, covered in mud with a dripping wet rucksack, at her red brick terraced house. She let me in though and made me have a bath before feeding me with Yorkshire pudding.

I joined ULSA at the first opportunity. At Leeds many of the cavers had nicknames. There was a Minitrog, a Torchy, a Fritze, and a Ginge. Minitrog declared that I would have to have a nickname and he hit upon the idea of calling me Pooh. I was appalled. This was *not* a suitable name for a would-be caving superstar! I indignantly inquired as to *why* he thought this a good name. Minitrog explained that he could imagine me having hare-brained schemes like the A.A. Milne character, and doing things like floating around on balloons and getting stuck in caves through eating too much honey. I was adamant that this simply would not do and would he please not call me Pooh. Of course, this ensured that the name stuck.

More from ULSA Review 8, July 1971, Gasson's Series.
by Dave Yeandle.

At the entrance the two parties discussed their trips. Tony and Dave J had explored and surveyed 210m of the Thunder Pot Inlet passage but they found it hard to believe that the first of the dreaded grit bands had been passed and that Langcliffe was wide open again.

Following a night in Leeds to obtain sleep and tackle, the same group, plus Alan Brook, began the fearsome task of getting ladders to the pitch. It was a sunny day and nobody seemed too keen to crawl through a damp cave. Even Dave J had lost his usual resolve and though he was persuaded to go down he was later heard to mutter something about not having wanted to wait on the surface till dawn. Surprisingly speedy progress was made through the cave, no doubt because everybody wanted to be in front!

On reaching the pitch (Nemesis) a doubtful belay was found and Iain descended. He was not disappointed for once below the murderous take-off the shaft became stable. The ladder hung freely in a clean circular shaft of 6m diameter, and 15m below a ledge was encountered. A further 7m climb and the bottom was reached. Tony and D.B. descended in quick succession and followed the watercourse down through a very tight bedding plane squeeze into a passage with a bouldery roof. The stream was found to disappear a short way further along, and after another 12m a boulder chamber was reached. There was no obvious way on and it was clear that the explorers were at the top of the second grit band; another boulder choke seemed the order of the day. By poking around in the boulders the stream was regained, only to find that it disappeared once more. However the hole through which it sank was diggable and prospects weren't too bad.

Meanwhile, back at the pitch, A.B., Dave J and Dave Y had been having light trouble! Eventually they reached the bottom of the pitch and made their way to the end, discovering that it was possible to avoid the bedding plane squeeze by climbing over the top of the collapsed block which had formed it. More boulders were moved from the choke before the cavers started back to the surface.

The following Saturday a small army of cavers stomped up to Langcliffe. The party included Howard Crabtree, Iain Gasson, Alf Latham, Mick Mulligan, Martin Rogers, Tony White and Dave Yeandle. Most people reached the 'end.' Even the mighty Alf managed to excavate his way into Boireau Falls Chamber. Tony and his crowbar were the first to reach the dig and together they forged onwards. While he worked, numerous people dropped in to shout encouragement: Howard however was not seen but growls were heard which indicated that he had almost made it. (Howard often growls in boulder chokes).

After an hour, only Tony, Iain and Dave Y remained working in the dig. Suddenly the silence was shattered by shouts of joy. The diggers were through and they negotiated the blockage into what turned out to be the most incredible boulder choke. A short way along, the tortuous path of the noisy stream disappeared into an impenetrable crack and the cavers were obliged to enter the wilderness above; a horrible jumble of loose gritstone and limestone boulders. The stream was eventually regained, only for it to disappear almost immediately. A way on was found though, and the going started to get easier and the cave dropped rapidly. A final squeeze down and out of the boulder choke and Langcliffe was beaten again. In front of the cavers lay a large passage situated in the Hardraw Scar Limestone.

It came as somewhat of a surprise to the explorers to discover that after only 60m the large passage just seemed to stop. A quick inspection showed that the stream could be followed through a short duck on the right, whence the passage again increased in size. It was a streamway of different character which led down steeply over a boulder strewn floor for 90m to a massive frothy sump in a large chamber, from which there was no apparent outlet. Poseidon Sump, as it was later named, was a completely unexpected and ridiculous end to the Langcliffe streamway. Furthermore, it was clear that its water level backed up by as much as 12m.

The three disappointed cavers made their way back through the duck and inspected the main passage once again. Their spirits rose with the discovery that the end had simply been illusory and they were able to proceed leisurely along a dry passage into more virgin lands. Pleasant grey walls had supplanted the oppressive black ones of the old cave and with the passing of seconds the noise of the stream with its dispiriting associations soon died away. Only the occasional boulder fall prevented the most rapid of movement and it was just after one of these that an interesting find was made. In a sloping chamber a strange fungus which resembled a spider's web, had spread itself over boulders. The area it covered was about 4 square metres and luckily there was plenty of room to pass by without causing damage.

The passage (Sacred Way) increased in size, but eventually progress was barred by a large boulder fall. The way on, a traverse over a drop followed by a short climb down, led into a collapsed chamber—the Agora—25m long and 12m square and 300m from the duck. On entering the chamber a white object seemed to be hovering in the air. On ascending a slope of boulders the source of the apparition was seen to be a cluster of formations. This splendid display of colour, by far the best in the system, consisted of a large calcite flow and erratic stalactites, some stained by a red mineral. Thankfully the whole mass was well up on the wall and out of the way of any careless cavers. The exit from the Agora was down a hole in an area of calcited boulders and while Iain and Dave Y fettled their carbide lamps Tony descended to another boulder slope, whence he was able to proceed along yet another large passage. Since the passage showed no sign of terminating after about 100m he returned to his two companions. A considerable length of time had been spent underground—indeed they discovered that they were now Sunday cavers and because of work commitments the party decided to quit the system.

The following Saturday saw D.B., A.B., Tony, Iain and Dave Y racing back down. The passage below the Agora was followed over gour pools and false floors along a high wide section named Aphrodite Avenue. After 260m the gours gave way to a massive boulder strewn passage, in which several squirms among boulders and occasional formations made progress interesting. The passage, Silver Rake, continued for 225m until it eventually decreased in size and a streamway was encountered. Downstream, a murky sump (Dementor Sump) barred progress but in the upstream direction a waterfall was climbed and access gained to an inlet passage (New Fearnought Streamway), which was reminiscent of Langstrothdale Chase. Followed for 230m the end was a solid choke of boulders in which probing had no effect.

A.B. and Tony set off back with the task of looking at all possible ways on, while D.B., Iain and Dave Y started to survey out. The survey was taken to the Agora and nothing more of any length was found by either party. The surface was reached after an eighteen-hour trip.

One week later D.B., Tony, Iain and Martin Rogers visited Langcliffe again and while they were down the stream sinks at Swarth Gill, Benfoot, Rigg Pot and Thunder Pot were dyed. Only the dye from Thunder Pot was seen and this entered via the Thunder Pot Inlet as expected. During the eighteen hour trip a draughting passage above the waterfall in New Fearnought Streamway was followed for a few miserable metres and the survey was continued back to Boireau Falls Chamber.

On the 25th July Iain made a solo 12 hour trip to the draughting passage above the waterfall and he was able to push on for a further 15m to a point where progress was impossible and the draught had disappeared.

On the 5th September another trip was made into Langcliffe. The main purpose was to detackle and while Tony and D.B. surveyed the Poseidon Sump Passage, Iain, Mick Mulligan and Dave Y made their way to Dementor Sump to recover ladders left from an earlier trip. The sump was closely inspected and found to be quite tight and sloping down at about thirty degrees to the horizontal.

It was me that had 'inspected' Dementor Sump because I had decided to dive it. I had yet to pluck up the courage to own up to this plan. I was sure that this was the way on; a short dive, I convinced myself, would make me the discoverer of the Black Keld Master Cave! All I had to do was to learn to cave dive, get some gear and get some people to carry for me.

I was keen to discover new passage in 'the old cave' upstream of Boireau Falls Chamber. In May 1971 Charles Yonge, Paul Everett and myself went up Thunder Pot inlet and after a short dig around a boulder at the end and after getting stuck for a while, I explored about 25m of horrible low passage heading for Rigg Pot. We emerged from the cave in the early hours of the morning and slept behind a wall near the entrance. After an uncomfortable night I descended Rigg Pot alone. I was hoping to connect Rigg to where we had been the previous day in Langcliffe. This was probably a futile effort as dye tests had indicated that the water from Rigg didn't even go into Langcliffe. I had however formulated some theory to get around this minor problem. I failed to convince anyone of the validity of my science and my companions refused to leave the glorious sunshine for the dubious pleasures of Rigg

Pot. In the event I pushed the final crawl for about 25m. A very tight wet passage it was too.

I returned to Rigg later in the year with Bob Greenwood. We travelled from Leeds in Bob's unreliable three-wheeler. He was very proud of his 'car' as very few undergraduate cavers could afford to run a motor of any kind. We often did midweek caving trips to the Dales when Bob had no lectures. Seeing as I didn't go to many of mine anyway, I had no trouble fitting in with his timetable. The top speed of this vehicle was about thirty-five miles an hour. Uphill our speed would drop to about twenty and we were responsible for causing long tailbacks on the winding Yorkshire roads. There were holes in the floor of this wreck and one could almost be tempted to try to speed things along, Fred Flintstone style.

Breakdowns were frequent and on this trip the chain snapped on Addingham Hill. Still, we made it to Kettlewell and, attempting to look like hill walkers, not cavers; we went and surveyed Rigg Pot. Dave Brook and Howard Crabtree had been trying for over a year to negotiate access to the fell with the landowners. They had not been able to get permission and I had realised that there was less chance of being caught trespassing if we approached the fell by an indirect route.

Until now I had always been Dave Brook's or Tony White's assistant while surveying and Rigg Pot was the first survey I had drawn and produced myself. It showed all of 150 m of passage and I was very proud of it. I managed to get my name on three times and hung a copy of it on the living room wall of the house I now shared with Dave Tringham, Dave Hedley and other cavers. I thought it rather complemented the left wing posters calling for the overthrow of both the Ted Heath government and capitalism in general.

My flatmates did not share my high regard for the Rigg Pot survey, and one night I came home from the pub to find that it had been defaced! (Underneath the official bits, like 'Surveyed by D.W. Yeandle' and 'Drawn by D.W. Yeandle' they had added things like 'Directed by

D.W. Yeandle,' 'Film Score by D.W Yeandle' and 'Concept Album by D.W. Yeandle.' They used pink crayon!)

In April '72 Paul Everett and I visited Gypsum passage, a dry inlet to the main drain. Dave Brook had told me that a dig in the boulder choke at the end of this inlet could yield new passage. I arranged to meet Paul in Kettlewell. As usual I planned to hitchhike from Leeds, always an unreliable means of transport for me, probably due to my shoulder-length hair and brown ex-army greatcoat. This day was particularly trying as no cars whatsoever would stop. This was perhaps because I was carrying a five-foot long crowbar along with large amounts of caving gear. Eventually I gave up and started to use local buses and even one of those refused to stop! Eventually I got lucky as Sid Perou and Steve (Tiny) Calvert (from the Happy Wanderers) drove past and recognised me. They gave me a lift to my destination even though this was well out of their way. Paul didn't seem to mind my very late arrival and as usual was amused at my incompetent hitch-hiking. (Paul was very good at getting lifts and had hitched all over Europe and the USA).

We eventually got underground after five in the afternoon, late even by our standards. At the start of the Kilnsey Boulder Crawl we decided to have a go at bypassing it by following the main stream. After sliding through one of the stream sinks we entered a hands and knees crawl. This developed into a walking sized streamway and after about 200m a climb gave access to the distant end of the Boulder Crawl. Pleased with our easy success, we quickly continued to Gypsum Passage.

After some rather frightening digging in loose boulders with our large crowbar, a hole was opened up and Paul was able to squeeze through and kindly enlarge the squeeze for me with a lump hammer. Paul then continued a short distance to another squeeze. He negotiated this easily and broke through to a large passage. I joined him quickly. By now our carbide lamps were providing only a pathetically small amount of illumination. Excited as we were at the thought of the exploration ahead we spent some time doctoring our inadequate lighting.

The passage continued large for 100m to a second boulder choke. By ferreting around we were able to pass the choke at a low level where we intersected a small stream. The cave was now smaller and after a further 220m of mixed walking, crawling through mud and squeezing through loose boulders, we ground to a halt. We had taken several minor injuries from unstable boulders both while digging and moving through the new passage. Also, our carbide lights were being very temperamental in the muddy environment and we wanted to get back to the main stream to give them a good cleaning. We named our new passage Crystal Beck Inlet.

I was exhausted and cold by the time we reached the Craven Crawl. My wetsuit was ripped in many places and I was hungry as our only food on this strenuous trip had been half a Mars Bar each. For a large part of the crawl I was hallucinating. To cut down on weight while hitchhiking I had decided to bring a ladder that was two metres too short for the entrance pitch. Going in we had simply jumped off. Reversing this proved very difficult in our exhausted condition. After much experimentation with combined tactics and an old sling we made it to the surface at dawn. We had made little provision for sleeping and simply lay down on the wet moor in our sleeping bags. We were too cold and wet to sleep properly and after a couple of hours gave up and went and dug in a shakehole near to Rigg Pot. I don't remember us having anything we could call breakfast, but it is possible that Paul had something revolting in the bottom of his rucksack. He was particularly fond of dry raw fish (still is probably!) and used to hang it up in the cellar of his Leeds flat. We were lucky though as that day the Happy Wanderers were digging in the area. While the lads dug, their girlfriends went for a walk and came upon a wild looking Everett and Yeandle. Alison (Sid Perou's wife-to-be) and Denny were a bit concerned at our condition and asked what we were doing up on the moor in such a state and why didn't we go home? We hadn't thought of this but decided it was a good idea. We walked over to Mossdale entrance with the girls, who kindly gave us some food, and then we headed towards the road and the uncertainty of hitchhiking. At least I had left the crowbar down Langcliffe.

Feeling our find gave me some credibility, I now announced my intention of diving Dementor Sump. I could not afford very much diving equipment but Steve (Tiny) Calvert of the Happy Wanderers agreed to lend me his.

I had first met Tiny (who is very large) in Ease Gill. I had not been long at Leeds and was with a party of fellow students on an ULSA bus meet. We were looking for County Pot. We didn't know the way and I was glad to come across another party of cavers (who I later realised were from the famous Happy Wanderers). I asked the way to County and Tiny gave me clear instructions as to how I could reach our objective. His directions were deliberately wrong and we got very lost and confused. He didn't like students! Over the next few months I often came into contact with the Wanderers. Mostly skilled tradesmen working in heavy industry, they had little regard for student cavers—perhaps because the Wanderers were often called upon to rescue students trapped underground or maybe just because of cultural differences. The Wanderers had immense respect for the Brook Brothers and Iain Gasson though. Whenever I met Tiny he would bait me mercilessly. I considered him an uncultured yob and would always respond aggressively, even though he is twice my size. Eventually we decided we quite liked each other and became good friends.

Now I had some diving gear I wanted to get some cave diving experience before my first exploration dive—at the end of Langcliffe. Alf Latham needed a back-up diver for a trip he was planning in Goyden Pot. The object of the dive was for us to survey the river passage beyond sump two and for Alf to do an exploratory dive in sump three at the end of the known cave.

On a Friday evening in April '72 a large party of ULSA cavers assembled outside of Goyden. The group included Chas Yonge, Paul

Driver, Paul Everett, Steve (Crabby) Crabtree and Martin (Ches) Davis.

I was not at all organised with my equipment and to my distress I found I only had one wetsuit sock. I had a conversation with Alf that went something like this:

"Ohh Alf, I've lost a wetsuit sock—can I borrow one of yours?"

"No Pooh! If you're going to be a cave diver, you're going to have to stand on your own two feet!"

We bypassed the first sump by Gaskell's Passage and we kitted up at the second. Amongst many bubbles and with much splashing around I commenced my first cave dive. I went first on a base fed line—the visibility was good and the passage quite large. I had little trouble passing the sump which turned out to be 10 m long with two air bells. Alf followed me through, we dekitted and started to survey towards the third sump.

The streamway was large and impressive and would have been easy to survey had our tape not jammed at 6m. Still, we surveyed 100m to the third sump. Alf kitted up and dived. He explored 30m of underwater passage to a point where the size of the bedding decreased. We exited the cave well pleased with our efforts. I was ecstatic at having done my first cave dive.

A couple of weeks later a large number of ULSA cavers descended Langcliffe. Charles Yonge pushed on into new ground in Crystal Beck Inlet, while Paul and myself surveyed into the Inlet behind him. Meanwhile Dave Brook and Crabby surveyed the bypass to the Kilnsey Boulder Crawl and then overtaking Paul and myself followed Charles into the Unknown. Charles had explored a further 200m, mostly a large rift passage to a third boulder choke. When Dave Brook and Crabby reached the end they surveyed back to join up with Paul and myself. Most of the party had nasty moments with moving boulders.

By now I had generated a lot of support for my Langcliffe dive. Alf had agreed to take me into Keld Head on a training dive. At this stage of the exploration of Keld Head the main way on towards Kingsdale

Master Cave had not been found, although Mike Wooding had pushed a low inlet for 300m. We were all in great awe of this achievement. Somehow the training plan got abandoned and I ended up setting off in search of the main way on in Keld Head. This was definitely over ambitious for a second cave dive! In the event my only light failed not far into the resurgence and I turned around and went out.

As a final training dive I went into the main sump in the S.E. rising of Nidd Heads. I had talked Ches into holding onto a base fed line. 25m in the line tangled at base and Ches gave the return signal. I did so reluctantly as I was enjoying myself and starting to feel at home underwater.

3rd June 1972: Seven ULSA cavers walked to Langcliffe entrance carrying ladders, ropes and diving equipment. The object of this trip was to carry as much gear as possible as far as possible into the cave in preparation for the actual diving trip. Most of the party declined to actually go underground and only myself and the always dependable Paul Everett set off down, carrying huge loads. We managed to get most of the gear to within 250m of Boireau Falls Chamber.

I planned to dive the following weekend. In the event the weather looked doubtful, so we postponed the trip.

17th June 1972: The weather was still unsettled but the forecast was good. I decided to go ahead with the dive.

Paul was now working as a salesman for a company selling textiles in Eastern Europe. He was doing very well at his job despite always being told off for turning up at his office in his Duvet Jacket and with a rucksack instead of a briefcase. On the Sunday of this weekend he had to go to Bulgaria to sell felt. He knew that he would miss his flight if he went with me down to the end of Langcliffe, so typically he kindly offered to do another carrying trip and take the gear on to Boireau Falls Chamber. He got Stuart Ingham to help him with this task and they set off very early on Saturday morning.

Meanwhile the rest of us were congregating in a Skipton transport cafe and eating large amounts of very greasy food. We knew that we were about to attempt the longest and hardest 'carry' in the history of British caving. The atmosphere was one of both apprehension and subdued excitement. I think most of my friends suspected that I was not really ready for exploratory cave diving. I didn't know this, then, and I was determined to go for it.

Once all the party had assembled and eaten, we set off to Langcliffe entrance along with a small number of other cavers who had turned up to wish us well and 'see us off.'

The underground team consisted of: The Brooks, Crabby, Alan Goulborne, Dave Hedley, Helen (now Davis) Sergeant, Mike Sutton, Dave Tringham, Tony White, Charles Yonge and myself.

Before we went down Dave Brook organised some of the team to divert the water from Thunder Pot into Rigg Pot. This later turned out to be a very shrewd move.

We made steady progress and just before Boireau Falls Chamber we met Paul and Stu on their way out. Paul said that he was very tempted to go on in with us and get the sack from his job. He wisely chose not to do this and the pair carried on out. Helen was not enjoying the trip and went out with Paul and Stu.

The first boulder choke between Boireau Falls Chamber and Nemesis Pitch proved to be difficult and dangerous with our large loads. Some boulders moved slightly and it took a long time to ferry all the equipment through to the head of the pitch. When at last we had completed this task, I descended the pitch and had all the gear lowered down to me. I picked up a load and set off into the second boulder choke. When I got to the original dig below the pitch I was horrified to find that it had fallen in. I could not even work out where to start digging so I called through the boulders to Tony to come and have a look as he was the one that had dug it open in the first place. Tony knew which key boulder to move and he did so with his normal efficiency. He then passed it back to Mike and myself. We could find nowhere safe to put it and in the end tied it up to another boulder with some diving line.

Tony now moved some more boulders and moved forward, only to find the passage once again blocked. He dug through this new blockage and progressed a short distance to yet another place that had changed. He returned to Mike and myself to discuss the problem. I now went up front and realised that two large boulders had fallen out of the roof, blocking our original route. I squeezed up over the top of these boulders and could see a way on downward and round a bend. It looked very tight but possible. However, I thought if the way was blocked further on I would most likely not be able to reverse the move. I knew that if I thought too much I would back down from this problem and I feared that the dive would then be abandoned. I breathed out and pushed myself down into the hole. To my immense relief I found myself in a passage large enough to turn around in, which I needed to do to negotiate the next bit. The way on from here was open and unchanged since my last visit. I shouted this news through to Tony and he started to organise the transportation of the diving gear through this dangerous choke.

We continued without incident to Dementor Sump, reaching it nine hours after leaving the surface. Alan Goulborne said, "Well, Pooh, this is your big moment." He sounded worried! The sump pool seemed more silted up than when I had last seen it and I couldn't find a good spot out of the mud to kit up. It seemed to take me a long time to get ready and Crabby said, "I bet Mike Wooding doesn't have this trouble!" My equipment included only one cylinder (45 cubic ft), only one regulator, only one light and 60m of line.

I started the dive with difficulty, flat out, lying in the mud. Once I was underwater I discovered the sump to be a bedding with about 30 centimetres between the mud floor and roof. The visibility was nil. At around five metres from base the mud floor dropped away and I found myself in a more roomy passage, with half a metre of visibility. I felt the dive was going well and then my regulator started to leak water badly. I tried purging the second stage with no effect while still moving forward. I became aware that I was swallowing water and not getting enough air. I realized I was drowning! By now the sump was quite roomy and I could detect both an upward and downward trend. I groped upwards instinctively; dully aware that maybe this was the last minute of my life. I glooped up into a small air bell, coughing and spluttering. I again tried to stop the leak by purging; but with no effect. I realised I could not continue the dive; indeed, I was not at all sure I could make it back to my friends. There was nowhere to tie off my line and nowhere to place the line reel. The walls of the air bell were caked in mud and I dug out a small ledge and placed the line reel on it. I took several deep breaths and started to fin back fast along my line towards base. The line had got pulled into a tight part of the bedding and it took me a while to find a way through. I managed to survive long enough on the air/water mix my regulator was giving me to make it back.

Everybody was glad to have me back safe but disappointed that I had not broken through the sump. Charles, who had thought to bring down a stove, brewed up some very welcome soup. We then started out. I was very tired and cold and soon dropped to the back of the party. I seemed incapable of carrying anything except the smallest of loads. I felt rather ill and despondent.

I slowly revived and by the time I was half way along the Sacred Way I felt quite energetic again and was thinking about what my next diving project would be. There seemed to be a very strong draught and I started to worry when I could hear the main stream at a point from which I knew it could not normally be heard. Further along the dry passage I came across Dave Tringham and Alan Goulborne lying down in the passage. They told me that there was a flood on and that Dave Brook, Charles, Crabby and Tony had gone ahead to look at the second choke. I carried on to the main stream to find that it had become a raging torrent carrying about ten times as much water as normal. Dave Brook and the others returned from the end of the choke and informed me that it was totally impassable in these conditions. Never one to miss a photo opportunity, Dave Brook got Charles and myself to help him take photographs of the flood.

We then went back 40m along the Sacred Way to where Dave Tringham, Alan Goulbourne and now the rest of the party were resting. We started our wait for the water to drop, huddled closely together to keep as warm as possible. We drifted in and out of sleep. I would doze off only to wake up feeling very cold. I would then move around a bit to try to get comfortable and eventually sleep again. In my wakeful periods I started to worry about some of my friends who were showing signs of hypothermia. I felt I was very much to blame for our predicament. I had seen some storm clouds starting to build up just before we left the surface. I had not cancelled the dive as this was to be my last chance before most of us left Leeds for the summer vacation. Also, I was very anxious about the state of the second Nemesis choke. Would the boulder we had tied up with diving line, or any other boulders for that matter, move with the force of the water and cut off our escape?

On Saturday night torrential rain had struck the Dales. The Happy Wanderers knew we were down Langcliffe and when on Sunday morning they saw that the Dales were awash, they became very concerned for us and went over to Wharfedale to see if we were out of the cave. On arrival they saw no sign of us and became aware of the vast quantities of water pouring into all the Langcliffe feeders. They set a rescue operation in motion.

Meanwhile, in Bristol, my parents were preparing to welcome me home. I had just turned twenty-one and they were organising a birthday party for me. All our relatives were invited and my mother was busy baking a cake and preparing lots of food. My parents were very proud of me being at Leeds University and were unaware that by now I had decided to drop out.

After about eleven hours of waiting, the flood had subsided sufficiently for us to consider having a crack at the second Nemesis choke. We didn't have much food left so in an attempt to gain as much value as possible from our limited resources we brewed up most of our remaining Mars Bars into a sort of soup on Charles's stove. Leaving most of the diving gear behind, we set off. Tony White went first with me close behind. Both of us were expecting trouble with the boulders and we were prepared to dig our way out if necessary.

Getting through that choke was very desperate caving indeed. Several boulders had moved blocking the way out. Most of these were removed by Tony alone, from below. This would have been a great piece of work in normal conditions—in a flood it was an incredible achievement. By this stage only two members of the team had working electric lights—and our pathetic little carbide lamps kept being blown out by the draught or extinguished by the water. Several of the squeezes sumped up when the larger people in the party went through them.

Tony and myself were very relieved to find that the boulder tied up with line had not moved. We were almost out of the choke when we heard a loud explosion. "What the hell was that!" I shouted over the roar of the water to Tony. "I don't know, maybe a rescue team is above us and trying to blast a way through!" he yelled back. "Oh shit no," I thought, "they'll bring the bastard down on us, for sure." I was frightened now. Here we were, ten cavers, winding our way through this horribly unstable, flooded boulder choke, most of our lights out, surrounded by spray, noise and loose sharp rocks—and to cap it all a bloody great bang and the whole place about to fall in!!

We just kept going and made it out of the boulders. Slowly and one by one the rest of the party emerged through the last squeeze of the choke. I discovered the cause of the explosion. Dave Tringham had been carrying most of our carbide in a large plastic container. This had blown up and burnt his hair. Although this had given him a nasty shock he was not badly hurt.

Everybody was greatly relieved at having gained important ground. Even so, our situation was still serious. Our carbide supplies were now barely sufficient to get us out and although the Nemesis pitch looked just about climbable, we were sure that the squeezes through the first Nemesis choke above the pitch would still be sumped. Once again we sat down to wait, this time in the Boulder Chamber above the second choke—a rather draughtier spot than the Sacred Way.

By now a full-blown rescue operation was in progress with both CRO and Upper Wharfedale called out. Cavers from the NCC, Happy Wanderers and many other clubs had laid telephone wire to Boireau Falls Chamber and established contact with the surface. The squeezes in the first Nemesis choke were indeed impossibly wet; not that this deterred Neil Antrum (Nelly of the Happy Wanderers), Kenny Taylor (also Happy Wanderers), and John Donavon (Donny of the Preston Caving Club). This trio dug a new dry way through the first choke to the head of the pitch. After descending the pitch they could not find the way on because of the vast quantities of spay and water.

This caused them great distress because they thought that all of the further reaches of Langcliffe were low and flood prone and they feared that the remainder of the cave was sumped and we were most likely drowned. They were in fact only 50m away from where we were sitting out the flood in the Boulder Chamber. They returned in desperation to Boireau Falls Chamber, leaving an ammunition tin, full of carbide and food, on the ledge of the pitch, hoping we would make it through and be able to make use of it.

When Neil phoned the surface from Boireau Falls, morale there slumped. Comparisons started to be made to the Mossdale Disaster and some Happy Wanderers hard men were moved to tears. Tiny told me later that he wondered what he was going to do now on Thursday evenings. He expected the ULSA club nights at 'The Swan with Two Necks' would come to an end now that most of the active ULSA cavers were gone. This was the problem—a large part of the club was in the trapped party and only we knew the cave beyond Boireau Falls; nobody else had been to the end.

Two o-clock Monday morning in Bristol. A policeman knocks on the door of my parents' house. The door is opened. "I regret to inform you, Mr and Mrs Yeandle, that your son is trapped down a flooded pothole in Yorkshire. A rescue party is in the cave but the cavers have not been found."

We waited in the Boulder Chamber, huddled together like penguins to conserve heat—but still getting colder and colder. We could see and hear that the water level was dropping and this helped us to keep our spirits up. After about twelve hours we decided that just maybe the stream was low enough to allow us through the squeezes above the pitch. Also, we noticed that the stream had become muddy and deduced that a rescue was underway.

On the ledge we found the ammo tin. It was more than welcome, hungry and low on light that we were. We had a feast at the top of the pitch. The water seemed higher than we had estimated and we couldn't understand how our unknown benefactors had made it through the first choke; surely the squeezes were still too wet to pass. Tony solved this puzzle when he started out through the boulders and saw a rope hanging down a not so tight and completely dry hole. Seconds later he was up into Boireau Falls Chamber and telling the anxious rescue party that we were all okay and on our way out. We were again fed and between mouthfuls of welcome food, we told of our experiences.

There was a lot of rescue equipment in Boireau Falls Chamber and it all had to be taken out. The least we could do was help. Soon the distinction between rescuer and rescuee broke down and we were a bunch of cavers on our way out to the pub. I gathered that the landowners were not at all amused by recent events and that the press and police were aware that we did not have permission to be in the cave. I considered this whole debacle to be my fault and I was wondering how I could stay out of trouble. I hit upon a 'cunning plan!' I would pose as a member of the rescue party and slip quietly away upon emerging.

Upon reaching the bottom of the entrance pitch I noticed a lot of equipment waiting to be hauled up. To affect my 'disguise' as a rescuer I attached as much equipment as possible to myself; a rope, a couple of ladders, a large empty telephone reel and an ammo tin. I tied onto the lifeline and shouted up to the lifelining crew that a member of the rescue party was coming up. I hoped that nobody at the entrance would know me. I climbed the pitch as quickly as possible and then got jammed in the entrance because of my large load. Harry Long was on the lifeline: he knew me and after helping me out on to the moor sent me straight off to a large tent where John Frankland, the CRO doctor, was examining our overdue party as we emerged. We were all found to be suffering from the early stages of hypothermia. It was lunchtime Monday and we had been underground for two days. I was amazed by the large numbers of people at the entrance; apart from many cavers and friends, there were several policemen and reporters from most national and several local newspapers. Both T.V. networks were represented. I found the transition from the stark and lonely underground world to all this rather shocking. Dave Brook ended up giving most of the interviews but the BBC 2 man had found out about me being the diver and I ended up doing an interview.

We were driven by police Land Rover to Scargill House, a Church of England community centre, where we were treated to a bath and a hot meal. While having his bath Dave Brook gave an interview to the Times reporter. We were asked by several reporters to pose for a group photograph which we were told would be published nation-wide the next day. Somebody commented that we looked more like an alternate rock band than a group of sportsmen. Indeed, our style was somewhat 'hippie.' Along with about half the party I had untidy shoulder-length hair. Dave Tringham's curly hair was pretty much out of control as well. Most of us were the proud owners of ex-army greatcoats and our jeans were mostly old and patched. Alan Brook was wearing his white operating theatre 'wellies' and had the longest, most bushy beard of the whole group. Dave Brook looked halfway respectable, but with his cloth cap and somewhat moth-eaten corduroy jacket, he wasn't really all that conventional in appearance!

I wanted to get to Bristol as soon as possible to make it to my twenty-first birthday celebration. Also, I was already a day late for a

new job as a labourer in a tobacco factory. Alan Goulbourne gave me a
lift to Birmingham and I got on a train for Bristol.

*"EPILOGUE TO THE RESCUE" or THE BROOK BROS. TRAV-
ELLING GOON SHOW. From ULSA Review 11, February 1973.*

    by Roy Holmes:

    *The following is a graphic description of an epic adventure of the
dynamic caving duo "The Brook Bros." together with their companions
of the ULSA consisting of Pooh, Christopher Robin, Eee Haw, Uncle
Tom Cobley and All.*

    *Pooh was the cause of all the entertainment when he announced
that before going into foreign parts to seek work, he was going to dive a
few Langcliffe sumps!*

    *The date was set and a preliminary trip undertaken to take tackle
part way in. Saturday 10th June '72 dawned murky as usual, the
weather forecast promised a little more rain. It was decided that there
wouldn't be enough water in the sumps to dive, so the expedition was
called off until the following weekend.*

    *Saturday 17th was fine but the previous weeks' rain made the
sumps a better proposition and the forecast was for more rain to come.
With the promise of sumps endless the party entered the cave.*

    *Eventually the far sump was reached, Pooh kitted up, went in 10m,
came back and said that was it. Due to mechanical failure, mission
was called off. Meanwhile up on the surface it had dropped dark, and
rain ensued in large buckets full.*

    *Sunday dawned still raining; by lunchtime no one had surfaced so
reluctantly the CRO were contacted, but as it wasn't in their area the
U.W.F.R.A. were handed the problem.*

    *U.W. called their team,—radio, TV, press etc. and by 18.30 all the
country knew the situation and cavers from far and wide set off, all
searching for the glory of rescuing the Brook Bros.*

    *In the cave by now it was obvious that the water had risen, due to
the fact that the Boulder Chokes were impassable. The cavers decided
to go to sleep until the water had subsided.*

    *Midnight on the surface saw the first rescue team back with reports
of Ginormous floods. U.W. by that time were thoroughly established in*

the garages belonging to Scargill House and a large contingent of C.R.O. were nearing the site. More Police were drafted in to keep the two rival factions apart, but the C.R.O. made their camp in the adjacent drive. Reconnaissance parties were sent over to U.W. at regular intervals with strict orders to observe and report. This lulled U.W. into a false sense of security. At first light C.R.O. made their move. Led by the four ton truck followed up by the Land Rover and canteen, within an hour they were entrenched on the lawns outside the garages.

Separating them from U.W. were two police cars and about five nervous looking Policemen. The situation looked ugly. Was this going to be it? Would U.W. be finally crushed under the weight of tackle, and marauding hordes of C.R.O. personnel? No, U.W. started serving breakfast as a counter attack. Beans, sausage etc. were served up completely outflanking the C.R.O. who could only retaliate with corned beef sandwiches. Even with choice of tea, coffee or soup it was obvious that U.W. had won the day! Meanwhile underground the trapped party had noticed the water falling, so they decided to come out, meeting the rescue party on the way. News of the sighting of cavers soon spread through the camps and elsewhere.

By 10.00 Monday, press cars were arriving by the hundred, backed up by TV cameras. The C.R.O. saw an opportunity to get their revenge on U.W. and drafted in more men. Jim Eyres came, had an U.W. breakfast, cracked a few jokes and departed. Mike Watson arrived, eyes gleaming with thoughts of making money. U.W. never stood a chance. Within ten minutes he had sold the sole filming rights to both BBC and YTV.

Another battle was looming, BBC v. YTV, but with YTV bringing in a helicopter and BBC backed down. YTV's plan was obvious, to capture the Brook Bros. and take them to Leeds where they would be displayed for all Yorkshire to see at 18.15; but because of quick intervention by the rescue teams, the plan fell through. So that was it. 48 hours of caving produced 10m of sump—and a helluva lot of noise!

The girl sitting opposite me in the railway carriage was good looking, in a prim sort of way and I thought that she looked like a librarian or maybe a schoolteacher. She kept staring at me and I became embarrassed. After a while, she broke the uneasy silence.

"Excuse me for asking," she said, "but have you just been on television?"

"Yes I have. Did you find it interesting?"

"Well yes, was it very frightening down there?" she asked.

"Very slightly, on one or two occasions," I admitted, probably not sounding very convincing.

She smiled and wanted to know the reason people went caving. I couldn't explain why as I didn't have a clue myself. Instead I told her of my dreams of discovering huge and exciting caves in the Dales and under distant mountain ranges; and how great it felt to be the first person into a new passage. After a while the train reached her destination and she got off. My 'fifteen minutes of fame' were over; nobody else on the train seemed to recognise me.

I made it to my twenty-first celebration but had a lot of trouble staying awake. I was not exactly the life and soul of the party. Just before I went to bed I mentioned in passing that I wouldn't be going back to University and had decided to go to Morocco instead.

Our photos did indeed appear in the papers, along with the usual calls from the uninformed, to ban or control caving. Unlike most cave rescues, where the media loses interest after a day, in our case they kept it going for longer. I did hear that the matter of our trespass was actually raised in Parliament. Eventually the fuss over a raggy-assed bunch of cavers died down. I suppose they found something else to cause outrage or frighten the general public with. (Like the increased threat of a nuclear holocaust or looming nation-wide power cuts—or something.)

We never did discover the 'Black Keld Master Cave' and for a while I was sad that I had no idea as to how I might enter this huge, unknown system. Then we all moved on to other adventures and left the secrets of Black Keld for later generations of cavers. This is fine and how caving works. One day I'm sure it will be possible to travel underground from Mossdale Caverns to Langcliffe Pot and then onwards and downwards to the Black Keld resurgence in the Valley below. I'm certain that this will be one of the hardest and finest caving trips in the world.

2

Nasty Sumps

The official at the British Embassy in Tangiers seemed bored with our story and passed us on to his assistant. "Two more Hippies here Carruthers! Lost passports, as usual, sort them out old chap."

Carol and myself had foolishly left the bag containing our passports and most of our money unattended while on a Moroccan train. The bag had been stolen and now we were clearly nearing the end of our North African adventure. Carruthers explained that as it was now Friday we would have to wait until after the weekend before he could issue us with temporary passes that would allow us to return to Europe and the UK.

As we were leaving the building we were approached by a middle-aged Englishman dressed in a smart business suit.

"Could you please spare me a few moments?" he asked politely.

My first instinct was to try to get away. I had already talked to two Englishmen in suits in one day and thought that more than enough. This bloke seemed different though and appeared to lack the superciliousness of an establishment figure addressing wayward youth.

"Yes, what do you want?" I replied.

He explained that he had lost contact with his son who was travelling in Morocco. He had not heard from him for three months and had travelled out from England to try to find him. Perhaps we had seen his son on our travels? Would we please take a look at some photographs to see if we recognised him?

Carol and myself dutifully looked at the photos and shook our heads.

"Sorry", I replied. "We haven't seen him. I hope you find him."

The poor man thanked us and wished us well on our travels. "Oh, we're on our way home now, we've just been robbed!" I added unnecessarily as we walked away. I immediately wished I had not mentioned this. I hoped the poor gentleman would find his son.

We spent the next three nights sleeping out on a beach, getting rather hungry. We were pretty much left alone by the locals, except by one Gentleman, who turned up at our camp with a large freshly caught fish. Things appeared to be looking up.

"You like fish?" he said.

"*Schocron*, thank you," we replied, with relish.

"First, I have nice time with girl," he said, leering at Carol.

"Certainly not!" I replied, trying to sound indignant, although by now we were used to this sort of request!

"Okay, no problem—I have nice time with you", suggested our amorous visitor. It was now Carols' turn to say "certainly not!" She just laughed and took what I thought a rather long time to defend my virtue!

We tried to talk our visitor into giving us his fish for free, no sexual favours granted whatsoever! But he would have none of this and soon went away; libido unsatisfied.

There was a beautiful sunset that evening and as we sat watching it, my mind drifted back and forth over the long summer that was coming to an end.

My abortive dive in Langcliffe had been followed by six weeks of working in a tobacco factory in Bristol to get the money I needed to go to the Pierre St Martin with ULSA and then to continue south to the Sahara Desert. The PSM was at that time the deepest cave in the world and we had planned to make it deeper still. The Sahara seemed like a good idea. I was fairly sure that it wasn't all that far south of a place called Marrakech that I wanted to visit, because I liked a song called *Marrakech Express* on an Album by Crosby, Stills and Nash.

We had made it to the edge of the Sahara and I had enjoyed doing some of the hippy sort of things that young people did in Morocco in the early seventies. I was bored now though and wanted to do some more caving.

"Come back, Pooh!" said Carol. "You looked like you were miles away!"

"Yes, I want to get back to the Dales as soon as I can."

"Oh Aye, so you can dive more Nasty Sumps?"

"I know it's around here somewhere! I'm sure we'll find it soon." Brian Woodward and Phil Collett were not impressed by my supposed confidence. We had been wandering around the moor in dense mist for more than an hour, trying to find the entrance to Tatham Wife Hole. This was not a promising start to our diving project. Ferdy Walker and the ULSA support party were complaining about having to walk around in circles, carrying heavy items of caving and diving equipment.

"Hello! Hello!" a voice called through the mist.

"Over here!" I called back. "Is that Crabby?"

"Yes, what are you doing over there, Pooh?" A figure wearing a black trench coat, large wellies and a very silly woollen hat appeared out of the mist. "You're nowhere near the entrance; do I have to do everything? Follow me." With a theatrical flourish of an arm, indicating the direction we should walk, he stormed off, saying, "All you had to do was follow the fault line!"

What an embarrassing start to my plan of returning to Yorkshire caving and pushing sumps!

I was now living in Bristol and working on a building site with a gang of Irish labourers. Carol and I had arrived back from Morocco, impoverished and I had found this relatively well-paid job in order to enable me to buy diving gear. I wanted very much to get going with sump exploration in the Dales. I believed that contrary to popular belief the potential for original exploration of 'dry caves' through the diving of relatively short sumps was huge and that cave diving in Northern England, far from being nearly over, had in fact yet to start properly. After my near fatal dive in Langcliffe I recognised that I needed to get some cave diving training and I had joined the Southern Section of the Cave Diving Group.

I had started to turn up to training sessions organised by Oliver Lloyd at the University of Bristol Pool. Oliver had a reputation for being devious, rude and elitist. (In the back room of the Hunters' people sang caving songs about these supposed Lloyd characteristics). Well maybe, but I always found him pleasant and kind and he gave me and many other young cave divers a lot of his time and was clearly very committed to giving us a good chance of actually staying alive while doing an extremely dangerous activity. Oliver Lloyd was definitely eccentric though! He had a refined, old-fashioned English accent, wild curly hair and a dress sense that would have stood him in good stead at an audition for the part of Dr Who. Apart from all this he was an accomplished musician and academic. As well as my pool training I was able to dive as a trainee at Wookey Hole. I never went far beyond the ninth chamber (which in those days was not part of the show cave and was only accessible to divers) but nonetheless I was thrilled to have the opportunity to dive at this magnificent and historically rich site. John Parker, who was at that time pushing an amazing number of sites in South Wales as well as at Wookey, used to do a good job of making sure I didn't get myself in too much trouble.

I became friends with Pete Moody of the Wessex Cave Club and I started to dive with him in Swindon's Hole. On one of these trips I fulfilled my ambition to go to the end of the Swildon's streamway at Sump 12. On the same occasion I helped him push onwards for 30m at the end of Desolation Row. It was during this period that I first met Geoff Yeadon, in the University of Bristol Students' Union Bar, after a training session. I had the feeling that I had met him before and yet I could not quite place his craggy face, huge grin and striking resemblance to Mick Jagger. He suggested that maybe I had met his brother John. Oh yes, I knew John. I had caved with him in the Gouffre Berger and seen him many times on Newby Moss with his Kendal Caving Club mates. Usually dressed in para-military style clothing (but with long hair) they charged around the moor in Jeeps full of ladders and ropes in what would now be considered a totally environmentally incorrect manner.

Geoff explained that he was an art student at Corsham College, near Bath, and that his friend Bear (Oliver Statham) had done some cave diving in the Dales. Geoff said that once he had learnt to dive and finished his degree he was planning to dive with Bear. He invited me over to a disco at Corsham that very night and we set off in his very disreputable Morris Minor, of which he was obviously most proud! In high spirits on our drive to Corsham we enthused over this and that—of the merits of Chinese food, of rock music and of willing female art students we would surely meet at the disco. Also we talked a lot about cave diving and the amazing things just waiting to be done in the Dales. That night we got drunk and I spent the night on the floor of his student flat. Like everybody, I took an instant liking to Geoff and we became friends.

After a few months of training I felt I was ready to start pushing sites in the Dales. I mentioned to Brian Woodward and Phil Collett that I very much wanted to push Tatham Wife Hole. They agreed that it was a good prospect. I rang up Crabby in Leeds, who said he would organise some support. I was very excited about being 'back in business in the Dales.'

Getting lost in the mist was not an auspicious start to our Tatham Wife project but things seemed to be improving as Crabby quickly led us to the entrance. He explained that his late arrival was due to unforeseen problems hitch-hiking from Leeds. We descended this fine sporting cave very quickly and I was soon kitting up at the final sump. My gear included only one forty cubic foot bottle, one regulator, one light (an old Nife Cell) and 100m of line on a reel. This was November 1972 and this was the crazy way we dived sumps back then.

The Tatham Wife sump had been dived once before by Pete Kaye in 1968. He had gone in for some 12m to a silt bank, apparently blocking the passage. I dived and found the sump to be very spacious and only 2 to 3 metres deep. I soon encountered the silt bank and at first it looked like the sump was completely blocked. I swam up to the roof for a closer look and noticed a small hole between the roof and the silt. I just managed to squeeze through to a slightly larger continuation. I knew for certain I was breaking new ground now and moved forward quickly to stay ahead of the clouds of silt I was stirring up. After another 15m I was thrilled to surface in an airbell. Splashing triumphantly on I again submerged and after a further 20m of awkward tight sump once again broke surface. This was no airbell, I could hear running water and I could see the roof rising. I was through and in a virgin stream passage! I could not find a good place to tie off my diving line and for want of anything better tied off to a couple of muddy, fragile stalactites.

I crawled down the streamway looking for a good place to de-kit. I soon found a comfortable place to do this where the passage became larger and I could see a high level tunnel offering an alternate route to the low streamway.

Quite convinced I had broken through to 'Caverns Measureless' I excitedly started to strip off all my diving gear as fast as possible; leaving it in an untidy heap, I set off down the streamway. This turned out to be mostly hands and knees crawling with a low section, which I discovered I could bypass by a larger dry high level. I explored about 150m of passages to a point where the stream sank into a boulder choke with no obvious way on. I could see that the cave continued at a high level. I was finding it difficult going with no boots and my only light was starting to get dim and flicker alarmingly. Now that the initial excitement of the breakthrough was wearing off I started to feel rather lonely and 'out on a limb.' I headed back to my diving gear and got ready to dive back to base.

The visibility in the sump was nearly nil due to the silt and mud I had stirred up on the way through. It seemed tighter than on the way in. I soon came to a complete halt and realised I was jammed. The line must have got pulled into a different part of the sump to my original route. I was going the wrong way! I tried to reverse and discovered to my horror that I couldn't move in that direction either. Not knowing what to do and getting panicky I started to thrash around and over breathe. "I'm going to die for sure this time," I thought. "No you're not," said a quieter voice from somewhere else in my head. "Calm down, slow your breathing and find out where you are stuck." I obeyed: I stopped blowing huge bubbles and started to move my right hand, which was not immobilized, over the parts of my equipment and body it could reach. I soon realised that my bottle was jammed. By forcing myself in a sideways direction while at the same time holding the first stage of the regulator and shaking it as hard as I could, I freed the trapped bottle. The sump seemed larger to my right so I slowly shuffled over and to my immense relief found myself in a larger passage with visibility of about 50 centimetres. "Luxury! Not quiet dead yet—let's get out of here."

I quickly swam back out to base. As I had been away for much longer than my meagre supply of air could have sustained me underwater, my friends were relieved to see me back. I told of my exciting finds beyond the sump as I dekitted. I noticed that Brian was looking at me suspiciously and I asked him what was up.

"Dave, what have you done with my line reel?" he replied.

"Well I had it when I started back. I don't really know what has become of it. Err...to be honest, I did have a slight epic in the sump. Perhaps I accidentally dropped it. I'll get you another one, honest."

Brian just looked disgusted and pointed out that I also seemed to be short of a fin. This upset me just as much as the loss of the line reel as I had only recently purchased this new pair of fins from my hard earned wages on the building site. Phil now joined in the conversation in his usual jolly way.

"Excuse me for interrupting with a minor detail, but the water seems to be rising. Perhaps when we have finished discussing how much gear Dave has lost we could set off out."

He was right and we exited the cave in very wet conditions with some of the lower sections only just passable.

The next day, before we set off to Bristol, I dived for my second time in Keld Head. Exploration at this site had hardly begun. Mike Wooding had dived to 300 m, mostly in a low side passage. I did not have any knowledge of what happened to the main line. On my first dive, a few months previously, I had only managed to go in a few metres before light failure had forced me to abandon the dive. This time I did a bit better and followed Wooding's line for about 100m, where I reached a pot. I found I was too buoyant to get down this as I was wearing no weights. After one or two attempts at descent, followed by rapid uncontrolled ascents to roof level, I gave up and swam back to the entrance. There were two other lines, apart from Wooding's line belayed at the entrance. I followed one of these a few metres to where it ended, decided it was useless and removed it from the sump. I then followed the remaining line. This turned out to be the main line. It took me to an airbell at 45m and there it just stopped. I was astonished by the size of the sump and exited in awe.

Two weekends later and Phil, Brian and I were back up from the South. We planned to all go through the sump, equipped with boots, surveying gear, food (Mars Bars), rope and what passed for SRT gear back in 1972. We were prepared for a long exploration trip and anticipated dramatic finds. We were fortunate that a chance meeting with Martyn Farr in Bernie's Cafe lead to him offering to ladder up the pot for us, assisted by another Welshman called Howell. This helped ease the burden of the carry in. This time we had no carriers and three sets of diving gear, so it was hard work getting to the sump. We were enjoying ourselves though, with Phil and Brian making imaginary bets on which items of equipment I would lose or destroy on this particular trip.

We were a bit worried about the possibility of a flood. We had experienced trouble on the M6 motorway while driving through torrential rain. As a precaution we kitted up at the bottom of the final pitch instead of further in at the end of the canal. This was based on the idea that we could dive back along the canal, should it get very wet or even sump up in places. We all passed the sump easily but I was very unhappy on emerging at the far end to discover that I had yet again lost one of my fins. Phil and Brian chuckled at this continuing inability of mine to hang on to my gear. Getting defensive, I suggested that I couldn't be all that useless as I had after all passed this sump in the first place. Brian just made some comment about me being barmy.

We followed the stream to the boulder choke and confirmed that there was no way of following the water through the boulders. We now entered the high level continuation I had noted on the first trip. Initially we were excited as this high level appeared to be a spacious passage and we had visions of it continuing easily for thousands of metres. We were very disappointed when after only eighty metres we came to a solid mud choke. Also the walls of the passage were rather worryingly coated with a black clammy mud similar to the mud in High Level Mud Caverns in Mossdale. We all agreed that this was an oppressive place that looked as though it flooded to the roof in places. We called it Raven Way and started to survey back out.

When we were nearly back to the stream we noticed a possible inlet entering from a cross joint in the roof. We couldn't climb up to this but were able to follow water emerging from the cross joint down through boulders to a continuation of the main stream beyond the point we had previously reached. I could feel a draught coming out of the boulders and thinking that again the way on was open set off downwards, feeling once more optimistic. I was disappointed when once again the choke became impassable and I could see no obvious place to dig. We ferreted around in the roof above the boulders and uncovered a bedding plane passage heading back upstream. It was very tight and muddy and we did not manage to follow it to a point were we could say for sure that it ended.

While Brian and myself carried on surveying back towards the sump Phil went on ahead to explore a large rift passage he had noticed on the way in. Somehow I had crawled past it three times and not seen it. I did not believe in its existence until we caught Phil up and he pointed me at this black space. "What! How can this be, how could I miss that! How far does it go?" Phil replied that he had been a few metres along and got bored. "Bored!" I immediately dropped the survey book, which anyway was starting to bore me, and shot off into the rift. Brian, infuriated by Phil and myself's buffoonery, drafted Phil into the survey while I thrashed off into more virgin passage.

I followed the rift at a high level for 50m to a tight upward section where I found I had insufficient energy left to make progress. I then reversed my steps and managed to find a continuation at a lower level. The passage was quite spacious with many boulders jammed across the rift. Some of these moved or went crashing to the floor when I stepped on them. After 80m or so I reached a small chamber with a stream entering from an impenetrable choke.

Well pleased with my efforts and now tired I rejoined my friends. We finished off the survey and swam back through the sump. On the way out of the cave we met Dave Brook and Crabby. They had been surveying and exploring in North Branch Inlet. They kindly gave us weary divers a hand carrying out our three sets of diving gear. It was late when we emerged and walked back down off the cold, damp moor. We were a bit miserable knowing that we had missed the pub and we were very cold and hungry.

Our spirits lifted when we reached the car to find that Janet Woodward had brought us pies and beer. As we tucked into these dainty treats, Phil merrily announced that he had a name for my 'non-existent' rift—Invisible Rift, and we could call the whole of the new cave beyond the sump FDS series (short for Freeze Dried Sump).

It was to be a few months before I did any more caving in the Dales. Back down south I did several more short dives in Wookey. My far point at this stage was only Wookey 15 and I very much wanted to get to Wookey 20 as this was then considered to be a long dive from the dive base in the Third Chamber. On one of these occasions I had to wait for some UBSS divers to return from Wookey 22, which was at that time the limit of exploration. I was hoping to be able to borrow one of their bottles so I would have sufficient air to have a crack at diving to 20. There were a lot of people diving in Wookey that day and the whole thing was being run by Oliver Lloyd in the Third Chamber. Apart from despatching the UBSS on their various missions he was preparing two art students from Corsham College for their first ever cave dive. One of these students was Dave Timmins and the other was Geoff Yeadon. Oliver was sending them on a base fed line between the third and second chambers. I wandered over to watch just to kill some time. Geoff did not look much like a trainee. The whole business of kitting up underground which usually was such a kerfuffle to most of us, appeared to be second nature to him—as if he had been doing it for years. I watched him enter the water and he just seemed to do it better than the rest of us. Instead of thrashing off with much splashing and blowing of bubbles, he elegantly slid in to the water and slowly and quietly disappeared.

Getting together the money to travel from Bristol to the Dales with diving gear was a problem for me at this time. I had moved back in with my long-suffering and very supportive parents. I was living as cheaply as possible and trying to save up enough money to rent a flat in Leeds. So I was very pleased when I received an unexpected telegram from the BBC, which presented an ideal opportunity for me to actually make a profit out of a trip up North.

Sid's film about the PSM was near completion it seemed. However, the BBC needed to get some extra background sound and film clips. They wanted various members of the team assembled in Leeds that Friday. Typical of the media, they expected us cavers to turn out at very short notice and work for free and at our own expense. I rang them up and said that if they wanted me to be there I would need to be compensated for losing twelve hours wages at the factory where I was now a labourer on the night shift. Also, I would need to be paid travel expenses. They agreed to what I considered to be a good deal and in glee I contacted Geoff Yeadon to offer him a cheap trip up North if he and his Morris Minor were available. Geoff was very keen and Pete Moody was too. Very soon we were on the motorway, heading north.

Chris Brasher (of four-minute mile fame) was working for the BBC then and he had rather innovatatively arranged for us to be given lots of alcohol at BBC Leeds while doing the sound clips. The plan was to get us to loosen up a bit and forget about the stiff upper lip and British understatement nonsense—which even then was still widespread among British cavers. He aimed to get us to talk about how we actually felt about caving. I think what he actually got was a good party as several cavers turned up who had nothing whatsoever to do with the film (once word got around about the free booze!).

The producer also wanted to get some film of us pretending to be in France at the PSM campsite in Saint Engrace. We arranged to do this in Kingsdale on Sunday afternoon. This fitted in very well with plans made by Geoff and myself to dive in the Kingsdale Master Cave.

Geoff had now teamed up with Bear and they had chosen to 'have a look' at an inlet sump believed to come from Bull Pot and situated shortly upstream of the Rowten Sump. I wanted to explore a possible right-hand branch in the first sump of the Mud River Series and also to have a look at the passage leading to 'the Deep Rising.' Geoff, Bear, Pete Moody and myself all set off underground together on Sunday morning. While Pete waited for me at the start of my sump, Geoff and Bear carried on upstream in the Master Cave to their site.

My chosen site had first been dived by John Ogden in 1966. After about 30m of spacious underwater passage I came to an apparent Y junction. I followed Ogden's line along the left-hand wall and after another 30m surfaced in a spacious streamway. I followed this for about 250m to another sump which I believed was the start of 'The Deep Rising.' I supposed that only Ogden, Frakes and Boon had previously been this far and I felt very proud to be at what I considered to be one of the frontiers of British caving.

I was too young to have known Ogden and Frakes who had been members of the group of six superb Leeds cavers so tragically drowned in Mossdale in 1967. Dick Ellis of the Happy Wanderers had one night in a pub amused me with stories of their mad antics on a Northerners' visit to Swindon's. The details elude me now and were perhaps slightly exaggerated in the first place by Dick; but it seemed that Ogden and Frakes had delighted in jumping off the ladder while descending the Forty Foot Pot in Swindon's. This was in order to show off to the Mendip cavers and prove just how hard they were compared to the supposedly soft southerners. I would very much have liked to have known these blokes.

Leaving 'The Deep Rising' for another day, I set off back to the first sump. On the way back to base I did a thorough search for the right-hand branch I had seen enticingly marked as unexplored on the Kingsdale survey. I entered a previously unknown airbell and explored several loops to the main passage. However, I always ended up back at Ogden's line and concluded to my disappointment that the right-hand branch did not exist. I arrived back to a cold Pete Moody and we quickly exited the cave.

I arrived late to the filming and sound recording session which was taking place at the start of the drive up to Braida Garth Farm. For reasons of continuity the BBC wanted me to shave off the beard I had grown since the PSM trip. I did not want to do this but in a moment of entrepreneurial inspiration said I would comply if they would increase my expenses. They refused and an argument followed. I still had not received any of the money promised me in the first place and I demanded it there and then. They paid up and I started to stuff the small wad of ten-pound notes into my wallet, feeling very smug. Geoff, who had by now arrived back on the surface, saw his opportunity and reminded me that I had yet to cough up his promised share of the BBC loot. After some haggling I duly paid Geoff and the filming of D.W.Yeandle, temperamental starlet, finally got underway; beard still in place. The group of cavers who had turned up to witness this farce were now treated to the absurd performance of me being 'shot' from several angles and positions in an attempt to under -emphasise the offending beard. During all this members of the Happy Wanderers kept interrupting, making rude comments and comparing me rather unfavourably to various Hollywood stars, both male and female.

When the Beeb had finished with me I went off with Tiny (Steve Calvert) for my first lesson on his motorcycle and sidecar combination—a large classical machine that he called 'The Starship.' Once I thought I had got the hang of motorcycling I headed back towards the film set in order to show off my newfound skills. I was obviously out of control and several people scattered in alarm before I eventually came to a jerky halt uncomfortably close to an expensive looking piece of sound recording equipment. I was asked to leave the location and not return.

Back down in Bristol I soon started to pine for the Dales and the wide-open sumps I knew existed. With hardly any money saved I packed up my caving and diving equipment and a few clothes and got on a train for Leeds. Dossing on various cavers' floors I soon had myself fixed up with a job in a factory; working on a production line making gas cookers. On the strength of this employment I was able to obtain a basement flat in Kensington Terrace, Leeds 6. I thought it was really good as I had all of three rooms for my exclusive use, with plenty of space for storing gear. On the downside it was very damp and most nights the kitchen was invaded by slugs which I had to duly evict. Never mind, the rent was very cheap and with my wages from the factory I could afford plenty of beer and a curry at one of the local Indian restaurants every night if I wanted.

Several people were at this time investigating the sumps at the bottom of Gavel Pot. In April 1973 I helped carry for Alf Latham and

Bear who were planning to push the upstream sump. The carrying party was large and well-organised and included Dick Ellis, Neil (Nelly) Antrum, Dave Cobley and John Southworth—all of the Happy Wanderers. Bear had problems with a leaking regulator and after 30m returned to base. Alf continued past the limit of exploration reached by Phil Collett and surfaced in a narrow passage after a dive of 110m. The passage sumped almost immediately. He tied his line off here and returned to us at base.

I liked the look of this sump: the water was crystal clear and Alf reported that the passage was clean washed, spacious and 'friendly.' The following weekend I was back, this time to dive myself. My support party comprised of Steve (Crabby) Crabtree and John (Donny) Donovan. We travelled as light as possible with only one 45 cubic foot bottle and a 10 cubic foot bottle. We quickly reached the sump and I was soon setting off upstream. I was very excited at the prospect of a wide open unexplored sump and as the dive progressed my confidence grew. The sump was indeed 'friendly.' I was bloody cold though. While putting on my wetsuit up on Leck Fell the zip had broken and I had improvised by lacing it up with some baling twine taken from the fence in the car park.

I reached Alf's bit of passage which is virtually just an airbell. I tied off my line reel and splashed off into the unknown. I was overjoyed that the sump continued even though I seemed to have entered a confusing maze area. After another 25m I reached the top of a flooded shaft. This was a good place to turn back considering my meagre supply of air. I peered down the shaft for a while to try to estimate its depth and tied off my line. I left my line reel on a ledge and started jubilantly back to the airbell, well pleased that I had pushed upstream Gavel. I was by now very cold and tending to over breathe. Suddenly I found myself surrounded by large air bubbles. "Oh no," I thought, "I'm losing all my air!" The training Oliver Lloyd had given me now came in really handy and I instinctively turned off my main air supply. Sure enough, the bubbles stopped. I now had a good idea of the cause of my problem and switched to my back-up air supply. I continued back towards the airbell as quickly as I could.

Upon reaching the airbell I removed the demand valve from the main bottle and saw what my problem was. The 'O' ring on the bottle's regulator had blown loose. I reseated it and replaced the regulator. To my immense relief the seal held. I had lost a lot of air and I was uncertain as to whether I could have made it back to base with a continuing leak and a partly used back-up supply of under 10 cubic feet. With no support diver at base, waiting and hoping for rescue was out of the question. The oxygen in the air in the small airbell would be long gone before help could arrive.

I swam back to my anxiously waiting friends with a rapidly dimming light. I was shivering violently by this stage and did not have enough energy left to get out of the water unassisted. My wonderful support team hauled me out, told me off and gave me food. My light then went out altogether.

When I had started caving in the late '60s the equipment available was very primitive and the choice limited compared to the superb products available in the specialist caving shops of today. This was particularly true when it came to lighting systems. It was common for peoples' lights to completely fail and it was accepted that on occasions one would be called upon to provide light to a member of your party; by regularly turning around and shining your light in the unfortunate person's general direction. The only available electric lights were ex Coal Board things. I'm sure these old Oldham and Nife cells were great pieces of kit when delivered new to the mines, but by the time the Coal Board had finished with them and they had been reincarnated as caving lights they were less than reliable. Cavers with greater technical skills than myself seemed to be able to keep their 'electrics' in good nick. I, in common with many cavers, could not accomplish this. Early on I had decided not to bother much with 'electrics' and relied upon the small carbide lights. These were of course always going out for numerous reasons including blocked jets, running out of calcium carbide or water or merely just being in a cave that was either very muddy or very wet. However, if one carried a few basic spares it was much easier to 'fettle' a carbide lamp than an 'electric' while underground. I became proficient at stripping down a carbide light in total darkness and then reassembling it and coaxing it back to life. Also, I was quite happy to climb ladder pitches in the dark if needed. In wet Yorkshire potholes this used to happen all the time. We would often just hang the ladders down waterfalls with little attempt to rig the pitches dry like we do now with Single Rope Techniques (SRT). So pretty early on in my caving I felt I had the lighting issue sorted and prided myself as being a 'carbide doctor,' no less!

All this was fine until I took up cave diving. Reliable underwater lighting was available from diving shops but it was bulky and expensive. So I tried to get by with various cheap 'waterproof' torches or my particularly unreliable Nife Cell which I almost never used for normal caving as even on a good day I could only get about two hours worth of light out of it. Usually I only used electric light while actually underwater. During the carry in to the sump I would usually only use my carbide light, in an attempt to preserve my dubious electric lighting for the underwater exploration ahead.

We then made a rapid exit from the Gavel sump. I reckoned the pot at the limit of my dive to be about 20 ft deep and that evening in the pub I passed this estimate on to Geoff Yeadon.

I have always kept a personal caving logbook. What follows is an extract from it, written in May 1973.

"I'm sure we can do anything," said Bear.
"I know," said I, "But what shall we do tomorrow?"
Shortly afterwards it is all decided: Skirwith Cave is to be pushed to caverns endless.
More Theakstons Bitter is consumed.
"Should be a two hour trip."
"Yeah, no need to take your carbide lamp."

An hour or two later and the sump is nowhere to be seen; the gear is very heavy and Bear is going on about "The brave companions continuing to battle on through the dark tunnels in an attempt to discover the secrets of the mountain and their inner selves."

The sump is reached at last and time for a rethink (chickening out). Eventually I reach the end of John Southworth's line, but don't want to push it anymore. Bear has a look at a rift in the second airbell and does sump one and two twice. That's that! Time to go out.

It takes ages and my light soon flakes, quickly followed by Bear's torch. After seven hours, we crawl out shattered, Bear's main light was nearly out.

I have always found keeping a log very useful. I soon forget the details of caving trips and dives so I always write up my log while events are fresh in my mind. I then have a record of events should I later want to write an article for a caving magazine or the Cave Diving Group Newsletter. Sometimes what is written up in these publications is a bit different from my log entry! For instance, this is what ended up in the C.D.G. Newsletter as a write-up for the dive in Skirwith Cave:

As reported by Martyn Farr (C.D.G. NL 27, p 10): Sump 1 (20ft) is followed by a 20 ft airbell; sump 2 (30 ft) by 30 ft of passage. Sump 3 (65 ft) to a 10 ft airbell, where Southworth's line is tied off. Sump 4 is choked after 80 ft.

The divers wanted to get to know these sumps and spent some time examining the second airbell to find a by-pass to sumps 3 and 4. Oliver climbed 10 ft up a rift and noted a passage heading over the 3 rd sump, but it was too tight to enter.

Makes us sound pretty professional doesn't it! It wasn't to be long after this trip that Bear actually started to get pretty professional. Me? I've still some way to go. I used to like to think that sometime early in the twenty-first century I'd eventually get my act together underwater. This has yet to happen. I miss Bear and imagine he would have laughed at my rather slow and erratic progress over the last quarter century.

Bear did have a great sense of humour and could do really good Adolf Hitler impersonations. At parties he would get up on a table; goose-step and do Nazi salutes. Like John Cleese in the Germans episode of *Fawlty Towers* he would hold his finger under his nose to simulate the Fuhrer's moustache and then rant and rave in fluent German. He would also do very funny impersonations of fellow cavers including Sid Perou, Bob Churcher, Watto, and even Pooh.

Shortly after meeting a well-known visiting German cave diver; Bear took him to a Dales pub to meet local cavers. All·evening Bear kept 'whispering' very loudly to people: "Don't mention the war!"

I was rather disappointed with my lack of drive on the Skirwith dive and wanted to redeem myself with a success somewhere. Martin (Ches) Davies was the local expert in the Nidderdale area. He had once mentioned to me that he wanted to connect Manchester Hole and Goyden Pot, and that the Pillar Pot sump in Goyden was very close to the downstream sump in Manchester. I decided now that this was an interesting project, especially as I knew from caving with Ches that he was very efficient at organising transport. (I still had not learned to drive.) In addition Ches was often willing to let ULSA cavers sleep on the floor of his house in Pateley Bridge if they were involved in one of his pet projects. His charming wife Sue would cook excellent meals for hungry and impoverished cavers. Yes, caving in Nidderdale could be . most agreeable and it made a great change from my normal weekends in the Dales—when if I were lucky I would end up sleeping in some barn or crowded caving hut, but more often than not end up dossing in a field or in a shakehole on the moors.

I contacted Ches and told him that I was interested in diving the Pillar Pot sump and was very pleased when he immediately offered to organise the whole thing—carriers, transport, bed, breakfast, evening meal, the lot!

My support party comprised: Ches, Dave Brook, Mart Rogers and a bloke nicknamed Nev. It was an easy and short carry as Pillar Pot is not far from the entrance of Goyden. As soon as we arrived, Dave and Ches set off out of Goyden, on their way to the downstream end of Manchester Hole. The plan was that if I broke through into an airbell or passage above water, I would shout loudly in an attempt to establish a voice connection.

I liked the look of this site. I could see clear static water some 3m down a 60 cm wide rift. There was plenty of space to kit up in and a really good belay for my line. I was soon climbing down the rift. I felt confident and ready really to go for it, even though climbing down to the water surface was awkward while fully kitted up.

Once underwater things became much easier and I was glad to discover that the rift continued downwards and did not get any narrower than the above water climb. As I descended the rift became more spacious and at a depth of 6m underwater I reached the bottom of the shaft. I now had room to swim around a bit and the visibility was about 1m. At first I thought there was no way on and then I noticed a small window in the wall of the shaft. I stuck my head into this and was thrilled to see that it went through to a black space. I managed to get my arms and then shoulders into the window and shuffle forward a little. This slot was quite tight but I now had my head into a larger passage and I badly wanted to explore it. Hoping my bottles would not jam I eased myself forward. Without too much trouble I squeezed my way through and emerged triumphantly into a 1m high passage. Happy that I was now able to turn around I swam forwards and to my astonishment after only 10m of horizontal passage I swam out into a large phreatic tube. The water was crystal clear. To my right the way on was choked with silt but to the left I could see the tunnel continuing. I swam off along it at high speed, feeling great. The tunnel was up to 2m high and 3m wide. I swam past several large pieces of trees that must have been washed in by floods. I became increasingly excited as I realised that the tunnel was gradually rising. A major break-through was imminent! Sure enough, 60m from base I broke surface. My morale slumped when I looked around at my new surroundings. I appeared to be in a very low airbell: the roof was coated with black clammy mud and I could see no way onwards. I did not think I had emerged in Manchester and had forgotten all about calling out, to try to establish a voice link. I now felt very lonely and noticed that I was rather cold. I could see no place to tie off the line and was thinking about what to do next when to my amazement I heard Ches.

"Hello, anybody there?" he asked.

"Well yes, its me," I replied. "Are you in Manchester? I can't see your light."

Ches now started to uncharacteristically yell with delight.

"You've done it! Well done! I know where you are…I think…don't go away!"

I definitely wasn't going to go away when there was a chance of me avoiding the dive back. I could now hear the unmistakable sound of a caver thrutching through a small passage. After a few more minutes, I saw a glimmer of light coming out of a tiny bedding plane. I was not at all sure I could get through and certainly would not have considered dekitting and entering this squalid looking hole had I not known that a Ches and a Brook were on the other side to help me.

I could hear Ches shouting back to Dave Brook now.

"He's come up in the static sump!"

Convinced now that I was back in known cave, I stripped off all my gear and pushed it into the squalid bedding. I then managed to get out of the water and start moving my gear towards my friends. I was able to make slow progress along to a very tight squeeze. Putting my head into this I was delighted to see Ches's bearded and grinning face. With relief I passed all my gear through the squeeze to Ches and Dave and then followed it through. It was a very tight squeeze and I had to breathe out completely to get my chest into it. I was committed by now though and just went for it and was soon climbing down into the Manchester Hole streamway. I was very pleased with this quick and easy connection. As I washed my kit in the streamway Ches took numerous photos of me. He kept going on about how much he was looking forward to drawing the connection onto his survey of the caves in Nidderdale. I in turn was looking forward to a square meal and perhaps even free beer back at the Davies' residence.

I was by now interested in returning to Langcliffe. I thought that I could dive the first sump beyond the Nemesis choke (Poseidon Sump) after a relatively easy carry, as most of the gear from my ill-fated dive in Dementor Sump was still in the cave at our first bivouac in Sacred Way. I talked Bob Churcher into accompanying me on this trip, having given him a glowing and rather inaccurate description of the cave. Even though we were not carrying a full set of diving gear between us we were rather overloaded on the long carry into Langcliffe. Bob took an almost instant dislike to the place. He is a big bloke and found the Craven Crawl and Stagger Passage most disagreeable. He kept muttering about how I had misled him about the level of unpleasantness of Langcliffe but he put up with it all stoically. After about five hours we reached Boireau Falls Chamber. Bob took one look at the squeeze out of the chamber and finally lost patience. He turned to me and said in his best army officer accent, "Dave! You are an idiot—a dammed idiot. How can you possibly have imagined that I could get through there? If you want to dive this sump you can jolly well continue without me. I'm going back out—this instant."

I had to admit that it should have been obvious to me that Bob could never have fitted through the tighter Langcliffe squeezes. "Err, yes Bob, I guess I've not really thought this trip out too well." Bob sighed: "No Dave, thinking ahead has never been a strong point with you."

I considered a solo carry through the horrible boulder chokes below us, and a lonely exploration dive. This I could not face so we went out of the cave together and not talking much. So we ended up carrying diving gear around Langcliffe for eleven hours, achieving nothing.

Once back onto the surface Bob forgave me and started to chuckle about it all.

Back in the early sixties Waddon and Davies had dived in the Nidd Head Risings using the old oxygen rebreather kit. I was particularly interested in the NW Rising and Alf Latham wanted to have a dive in the S.E. Rising. So on a beautiful summer day early in June 1973, Alf and myself made our way once again to Nidderdale.

Alf dived first in the S.E. Rising for a distance of 50m. He went in as far as the original divers and was unable to make any progress. We then went up the river a few metres to the entrance of the N.W. Rising. A short section of passage led to the first sump known to be 12m long. I passed this easily as well as exploring a branch to the right, half way through, to an airbell. So far, so good. I then found the start of the second sump 15m further into the cave. I knew that this sump had only been explored for a distance of 12m and I was confident of going further in. Sure enough I soon passed this limit and excitedly finned off into the unknown. At a distance of 80m I was well pleased with my efforts. The sump was for the most part roomy, although I didn't like the look of some of the piles of loose boulders I had negotiated. I returned in bad visibility and was relieved to not have any trouble following my line, as I was only wearing one bottle.

A few weeks later I returned to this site with Bear. We travelled over from Ingleton in Bear's latest motor, a rather old sports car fitted with a loud stereo system. We felt very cool as we charged down the hill into Nidderdale with Deep Purple at full volume. We both went through the first sump and then I set off into the second with two 40 cubic ft bottles. I passed my previous limit to a distance of 120m from base. I found the new section of passage very scary with numerous loose boulders. I was thinking about turning back and then to my horror my only light failed leaving me in total darkness. I immediately dropped my line reel and started to grope my way back out. I was terrified that if I encountered any line problems I would not be able to sort them out without a light. For very obvious reasons I kept a pretty tight grip on my line as I blundered my way outwards, frequently bumping into boulders, the roof and the walls. I was cold and this, combined with my fear, made it hard for me to control my rate of breathing. I did manage to keep my air consumption reasonable though, as I needed to do, with no way of knowing how much air I had remaining. I made a vow that if I made it back I would give up cave diving. After what seemed an eternity I saw a dull glow ahead of me. I was almost back to Bear and I started to relax a little.

I surfaced and in a state of shock described my dive to Bear. As planned he then dived.

He quickly reached the end of my line and after only 6m more surfaced in an airbell. With some difficulty he located the way forward through a tight slot in boulders and belayed the line. He then returned to me at base and we exited the cave. I lay for a while in the summer sun soaking up the heat and changing my mind about giving up pushing sumps.

That night we drank beer with Geoff Yeadon in the Hill Inn. Geoff was very amused to hear about my light failure and we all joked about how we would be lucky if any of us made it to the age of thirty. I didn't sleep well that night, though, and I realised that one day, maybe soon, my luck would have to run out. It did not occur to me that cave diving didn't have to be quite as dangerous as I was making it. I did realise however that I wanted more out of life than an early departure from the planet due to some underwater cock up.

Geoff and Bear were now starting to dive together regularly. I was to accompany them on a dive in upstream Kingsdale Master Cave. It was raining heavily on the day and we decided that KMC was very likely going to flood. So we went for a quick dive in Keld Head instead; reasoning that Keld Head was always in flood anyway, on account of it being a sump. We all went through to the (150 ft) airbell together and, finning to stay afloat in the deep water, took out our regulators to have a chat. We then half heard, half felt a deep rumbling vibration. "Bloody Hell!" At once we dived and headed outward. A few seconds after we all were out a massive flood pulse emerged from the entrance pool. We all laughed; Geoff and Bear had just done their first dive in Keld Head. This was July 1973 and British cave diving was about to change for ever.

That evening I went for a walk above Selside with my friend Nelly (Neil Antrum) from the Wanderers. He told me that he was soon setting off with his wife Denny and also Dick Ellis and Josie on a trip around the world. They planned to travel to Yugoslavia for a week of caving and then continue overland to India and Nepal. Then on to Australia to work before continuing around the world. He went on to say that they planned to trek in the Himalaya. I told Nelly that it sounded like a really good adventure he was planning. "Why not come with us?" he suggested as casually as if he were asking me if I would like to go to the pub. "Okay," I replied.

I had very little money so I started to work long hours at the factory to save some more for my trip. I did not stop caving or cave diving but I started to do a lot less—only going underground when there was no overtime available.

We purchased an old van for £50.00 and converted it to a camper. One final and quite mad dive in Border Sump in Stake Pot Series of Lancaster Hole was followed by a farewell party Denny had organised in the upstairs room of the Craven Heifer. After the party I held an auction of my diving gear in the pub car park. I was desperate to raise money and I let my precious equipment go for ridiculously low prices. I then retired to the van and our first night in our new home. Just as we were about to settle down to sleep, Jack, the landlord of the Craven Heifer came by and gave us a parting gift—a bucket of beer.

Departure day arrived and Geoff drove me from Kensington Terrace over to Dick Ellis's parents house where the van was parked. Geoff tried to tell me all about how he had pushed a sump in Boreham Cave; but I was too excited about starting my trip around the world to listen much. I had left packing to the last minute and my gear was in a state of total disorganisation. Geoff and Josie helped me load my stuff into the back of the van. I was most embarrassed when a badly hidden pack of condoms fell out onto the pavement. Geoff nearly collapsed with laughter as I made a futile effort to conceal this (hopefully) essential item from Josie. Josie saw though and although she tried not to, started to giggle.

Geoff looked ever so sad, standing in the middle of the road, waving us good-bye as we drove away. I wondered if I would ever see him again.

OPEC was starting to cause a fuss and the so-called oil crisis was about to begin. We were worried about not being able to buy fuel in Europe and stopped off at a service station to fill up all our empty containers with petrol. I suppose this was a bit illegal. We were stopped by police several times on our journey to Dover for minor problems like no road tax and no MOT. We were probably lucky to make it on to the ferry.

That evening, Neil and I watched the White Cliffs of Dover slowly fade from view. "Well Pooh, I wonder if we will ever make it back".

"I don't know, maybe—I hope so."

It felt a bit uncool, us going on like world war two conscripts heading for the front. We were supposed to be turning on, tuning in and dropping out, or whatever it was that increasing numbers of our confused generation were trying to do. I suggested we go below deck to the bar for a last pint of English beer.

3

Tales from Three Counties

The Three Counties System! It's almost a reality now in this new millennium. Just a few more links and we will have one of the longest cave systems in the world crammed into a few square miles of limestone between Ingleton and the M6!

I have been around long enough to remember when the possibility of a connected system of caves running from Barbondale to Chapel le Dale was almost too much for us to believe in. Dave Brook was the first to know—he invented the idea and the name.

In the late 1960s the University of Leeds Speleological Society (ULSA) used to meet on Thursday evenings in the upstairs room of the 'Swan with Two Necks' pub. I was an undergraduate in the physics department. Thursday evenings were special. I would watch *Top of the Pops* and then go for a sit-down fish and chip supper or even a curry at one of the cheap restaurants frequented by students. After that straight to 'The Swan.' Not only were these meetings attended by student cavers but also by members of the Happy Wanderers and Northern Cave Club (NCC). This was definitely the place to be for any ambitious young caver wanting a good caving trip (or two) over the coming weekend.

Dave Brook has never been an enthusiastic drinker and would generally arrive at the pub quite late. I thought of him as the best and most knowledgeable caver in the British Isles and I imagine so did most other people in our sport at that time. In any case, this diminutive figure—'Brooky or D.B.'—dressed in grey trousers, old tweed jacket with leather arm pads and wearing a flat cloth cap over a tremendously

unfashionable short back and sides, would arrive and quickly be surrounded by us younger cavers. We would be hoping to be invited on
one of his exploratory trips or wanting to ask advice on matters speleological. One by one, he would talk to us all and make notes in his small
red survey book. He would often give us hints of sites that "were very
interesting" or quiz us as to what we had been up to the previous weekend. Maybe we would be lucky enough to get to go underground on
one of his trips, or more likely, be pointed at sites he wanted to have
investigated.

It was at one of these meetings that he first told me of the Three
Counties System. I was at once thrilled with the idea and at the same
time found it hard to comprehend such a huge cave, maybe one hundred miles long, only 60 miles away from Leeds, in the Dales. Surely
caves this big were only to be found in faraway places like Kentucky or
Russia? Not just over the hill from Bernie's Cafe!

In 1969 much of the limestone in the Dales of the Three Counties
network contained only relatively short and isolated known caves.
There were some huge gaps to be filled and it took someone with
Dave's vision to see the possible links and indeed discover the Three
Counties System.

As I walked back to my lodging that night I was very excited about
this wonderful huge cave that Dave Brook had proposed. Even so, I
doubted very much that I would live long enough to see Kingsdale
Master Cave linked with Lancaster / Easegill.

Then a few weeks later the Wanderers broke through in Pippikin.

*PIPPIKIN POT—an account of ULSA activity in the system. From
ULSA Review No 9. 1972. By Dave Yeandle.*

*ULSA interest in PIPPIKIN Pot started in the summer of 1970
and it was during August that our first modest finds were made. While
Jake (Happy Wanderers) and Dave Howitt were discovering the Misty
Mountain Series, Tony White was exploring Ratbag Inlet. He followed*

the obvious passage and proceeded more than 400 ft further than previous explorers without reaching a definite end.

A week later, a large party of ULSA members entered the cave with the intention of having a good look around. Dave Brook and Martin Rogers visited the Hobbit and the Far Streamway. The other members of the party, Iain Gasson, Howard Crabtree, Tony White and Dave Yeandle followed the lower streamway down to the terminal sump in Waterfall Chamber. All agreed that the chamber was most impressive. Two of its noteworthy features were examined. The first was a low crawl in the opposite side of the chamber to the sump. It was followed in an upstream direction for about 300 ft until the airspace became limited; the ULSA had been up its first nasty, low Pip inlet—the first of many. The second feature examined was the waterfall; it had never been climbed. Iain decided he could do it and the 30 ft ascent turned out to be rather epic. Once he was up, a ladder was hung down and his companions followed in safety. Fifty feet of pleasant walking led to the base of another waterfall, beyond which the rift passage was choked with a wall of boulders. By ascending the wall for a short way and then bridging the upper part of the rift, Iain reached the broad, Niagara-like lip of the waterfall. The streamway was little more than five inches high and clearly impassable. (The stream in this passage is almost certainly the Cigalere water and the top of the second waterfall is close to the steam sink in Leck Fell Lane.) On their way out, D.B. and Howard surveyed the Entrance Series.

For the next six months, our visits to Pippikin were of a joke nature, but in April '71 Dave Yeandle accompanied Frank Raynor and John Thorpe (Lugger) of the NCC on one of their many trips into the system. Two minor extensions were made. Firstly, a hole in White Wall Chamber was descended and a small crawl entered which lead to larger passages. It transpired that the cavers had entered known cave by a new route! The crawl, Lugger's Link, forms part of Intercounty Passage which connects Red Wall Chamber with Ratbag Inlet. The second extension was near the Hobbit. A rift was climbed which lead to 100 ft of muddy passage containing a chamber and ending in a choke.

The following May saw another surveying trip, by a party of Wanderers and ULSA. Neil (Nellie) Antrum and Dave Brook and Dave Yeandle went up the newly scaled aven in the Cigalere. The passage was found to be spacious and sporting, containing many small climbs in water. The passage was surveyed and the final crawl was followed for a further 300 ft. (The survey showed that the Cigalere is 3200 ft long: it is the longest single passage in the system). On the same trip the Lower Streamway was surveyed by Ginge Hewson, Paul Everett and Howard Crabtree.

At Whitsun there was another Wanderers-ULSA trip into the cave. This time the intention was to have a good look at the Dickeries Inlet. The Wanderers and Dave Brook enlarged a hole in the downstream section of Dickeries, thereby discovering 100 ft of horrible passage: it was named the Red Rose Gallery as a sign of respect for our good, Nose friends up at Bull Pot Farm. While all this was going on Dave Hedley and Yeandle had started to survey the upstream section of Dickeries. In front of them Tony (the glorious), White and Paul Everett forged on into the unknown. Paul didn't forge very far and was soon found prostrate in the passage by the surveyors, who surveyed around him and continued. Just beyond an aven they met Tony who was coming back downsteam. He informed them that he had passed the previous limit of exploration (a duck) and had explored 250 ft to another aven. A crawl had continued beyond this for at least another 200 ft. The survey was to the far aven 'Dropout Aven.'

A few days later Paul and Dave Yeandle had to return to Dickeries to obtain six elusive compass readings. Accompanying them was Roger Bowser (a Himalayan explorer from I.C.C.C.). When their task was complete, they went to the Ratbag Inlet via Lugger's Link. Dave and Paul proceeded upstream: Roger went out in disgust. The final 200 ft of the inlet was surveyed. At the end a hole in the left-hand wall, five ft above floor level, gave access to a low crawl which lead to an aven. This they resolved to climb at the earliest possible date, even though it later turned out that the crawl had been entered previously. The following Sunday, the pair rose early at Braida Garth and, fortified by peanuts and crisps, they walked over to Leck Fell. The night before in the Craven Heifer it had seemed like a good idea to live off peanuts and crisps for a day, but with dehydration brought on by the early morning sun and alcoholic excess they became less sure of themselves, even though each packet of nuts carried the reassuring announcement 'extra protein.' They didn't get up the aven and developed a curious complaint, which among many things made them puke up. The trip was a farce, but at least a name now presented itself: Golden Wonder Aven.

On a trip in October '71, Dave Hedley, Dave Yeandle and Chas Yonge returned to Dickeries. Chas climbed 25 ft up Dropout Aven and entered 60 ft of passage ending in a choke. The remaining section in upstream Dickeries was surveyed—250 ft of disgusting passage and no conclusive end reached.

By November, people were feeling like another trip into Pippikin Pot, so Paul Bartlett (Sludge), Steve Crabtree (Crabby, a tamed Wessex member), Bob Greenwood, Dave Hedley (Torchy) and Dave Yeandle descended with the intention of scaling Golden Wonder Aven. This time maypoles were used and the team got up. It turned out to be 26 ft high and at the top 10 ft of passage led to the base of another aven (Andromeda Aven) which seemed at least 70 ft high.

It was decided that before any ambitious climbing projects could be sensibly undertaken it was necessary to survey all remaining passages in the Ratbag Inlet.

So it was that the following weekend saw Dave's Hedley and Yeandle back in Pippikin. With them were John Venn and Dave Tringham (two more tamed Wessex members) who went and dug in a passage near the top of the 12 ft pitch in the Hobbit; they broke through into a further 20 ft of rift passage.

Meanwhile the surveyors mapped the first left-hand branch of Ratbag Inlet, 80 ft ending in a 30 ft high aven, with an impenetrable bedding plane at the top. The second lef- hand branch was now surveyed. After 100 ft the passage split; the way to the right soon choked. To the left a previously un-entered bedding plane led off and soon developed into a typical Pippikin inlet passage, complete with pool, straws, false floors and mudstone beds. 200 ft along a choked bedding plane was reached but after a short dig the way on was clear again. A further 200 ft of very tight passage was explored, half of which was surveyed. A conclusive end was not reached. The dug out bedding seemed a little tighter on the return journey and D.Y. had extreme difficulty getting through. D.H. named the discovery 'Surveyors Dog Inlet' as a protest against alleged ill-treatment.

The following weekend saw abortive attempts to climb Andromeda Aven, although the survey was taken to its base. While this was going on Chas Yonge, Alan Goulbourne and Roger Howles took a car jack to the Hobbit and, using it to move a boulder from a bedding plane below the 12 ft pitch, they were able to enter 80 ft of new passage.

For a fourth successive weekend an ULSA party invaded Pippikin Pot. On this trip the maypoles were recovered from Golden Wonder Aven and a rope was left hanging down.

In January 1972 ULSA made its thirteenth modest extension to Pippikin. Those responsible were Tony White and Dave Hedley. At the end of the Far Streamway, a crawl on the left was followed into a series of climbs which rose to a height of 35 ft. On the same trip Paul Everett and Dave Yeandle scaled another 30 ft aven. This was located a short way up Ratbag inlet—it didn't go.

Over a period of two years the ULSA failed to discover a new passage in Pippikin Pot large enough to walk along and not an aven, a cross rift or the foot of a climb. It was felt that our toils were not completely in vain, for most of Pippikin is worthy of a visit and readers will now have a reasonable idea of those parts that are not.

During the early 1970s The ULSA had several digs going in the West Kingsdale System. They were all located in the series of dry passages reached from the Valley Entrance. The general idea was to find an extension heading west away from the Carrot Passage area and up towards Marble Steps Pot. Had we succeeded in doing this we would have gone a long way to filling in a major gap in the Three Counties System.

I did several solo trips into West Stream Passage and digging with a trowel managed to force another 30m along this flat out crawl in mud. In the end I gave up after becoming severely stuck for about an hour and exiting the cave, in a hurry, with a rapidly failing carbide lamp.

Paul Everett, Dave Hedley and myself continued a dig near the Roof Tunnel, started by Iain Gasson. This was a large phreatic passage completely filled with dry sand. As digs go this was a very pleasant undertaking. No water or mud and not even many rocks. It was almost like playing on a beach, making sand castles. However, there was one slight problem with this site. With no draught or ventilation in this dig, we did have a problem with carbon dioxide build up. After several visits to this dig, the problem became acute and we had a few incidents of diggers nearly passing out at the end. Eventually we abandoned the dig.

Caving was for me far more important than my studies at Leeds, and I often used to stop over in the Dales on Mondays. On these occasions I would sometimes do trips with Frank Raynor and Lugger. Ever since my first trip with Lugger down Pippikin he had delighted in every opportunity to 'wind me up.' I was very naïve even for a university student and I'm sure I represented an easy target for his piss taking. His favourite trick was to burn me off underground and leave me out of breath and confused. He was far fitter than I and a superb caver. I never had a chance of keeping up with him, although this didn't stop me trying. Frank was much more relaxed about things and would sometimes wait for me. He would often give me lifts back to Leeds.

It was on one of these Monday trips that I was lucky enough to be involved in a Three Counties Link. Baz Davies and the Manchester University cavers (MUSS) had opened up a pothole on Leck Fell which they called Big Meanie. (I think this name was chosen because of several incidents with large boulders causing injuries to diggers.) John Russum, who had invented the rock drill which had enabled places like Pippikin to be opened up, had turned his attention to a dig in a side passage down Big Meanie. Frank, Lugger and myself agreed to help him dig there one Monday in 1971.

The passage was drafting well and with unexpected ease we broke through to a pleasantly decorated continuation. Lugger rushed off ahead with the rest of us following at a less frantic pace, admiring the stalactites and trying hard to avoid damaging them with our passing. Very soon an excited Lugger shouted back to us: "We're into something big!" We all rushed along the new passage and about 70m from the dig came to a halt at the head of a pitch. We appeared to have emerged high in the wall of a huge passage. "We've discovered a huge master cave," I declared in my excitement.

Of course we hadn't. We had emerged 20m up from the floor of the main chamber in Death's Head Hole. Still, it was a nice find.

I was by now becoming increasingly interested in the Black Keld System and the deep caves of France; so for the next year or so I did less caving in the Three Counties area. I dived in Gavel Pot in April 1973 and reached the top of an underwater shaft that I estimated to be about 10m deep. This pot was later dived by Geoff Yeadon who descended for about 50m and it was still going down!

I had decided that I wanted to do some more travelling and started to work long hours and some weekends in a factory in Leeds making gas cookers. Before I set off on an overland trip to Australia with friends from the Happy Wanderers I did some diving in Lancaster Hole. I think Dave Brook can tell this story best.

The Border Sump. From ULSA Review No 12. March 1974 By Dave Brook.

After a long involved trial, with many false leads along the way, an underground detective serial is approaching its final episode beneath Easegill. Ever since the discovery of Pippikin Pot by the Happy Wanderers, and Stake Pot Series, by the Earby.P.C. a link between the giant Lancaster—Easegill System (19 miles) and Pippikin (4 miles) has been sought , thus joining two parts of the long speculated Three Counties System. This is not a tale of glorious breakthrough but of steady, patient and often unrewarding work by many people. When the link is established it will be on the backs of all who have contributed to this epic. Our story begins back in August 1971 when U.L.S.A.. began a grade 5 survey of Stake Pot Series to supplement the Red Rose re-survey of Lancaster Hole. It was complete apart from the muddy bits (such as Ramsden's Crawl and the Grind) when the E.P.C. published their preliminary survey at the end of August. There now seemed no urgency to finish our survey until the Lancaster work was nearing completion. If we had perhaps future effort could have been channelled in the right direction but also much information would have been lost or delayed.

The Grind and Echo Aven

Early in 1973 Cambridge University C.C. surveyed the Grind to the static sump which terminates the clean, deserted, downstream pas-

sage. *This sump was found to be below Leck Fell (as suspected by the E.P.C.) and very close to a tight inlet sump in Dickeries Passage in Pippikin. The Cambridge cavers thought that this would provide the long sought link between Lancaster and Pippikin but it must be pointed out that our survey data indicates that the Dickeries inlet sump is about 80ft. above the Grind and a hydrological miracle would be needed to make a connection. Echo Aven was known to lie on a master joint which passes through Sausage Junction, Ratbag and Cigalere. It was considered that a passage on this joint may link the S.E. end of Echo Aven with a high level passage in Dickeries explored by Chas Yonge. Andy Eavis, supported psychologically by Alf Latham, climbed 80 ft. up the S.E. chimney and found only a narrow choked fissure under the roof bedding plane. The major inlet passage could be seen at the other side of the aven but from its direction, inlets in Easegill around the Hairy Fissure may be its only feeders.*

The Border Sump Chapter I

The key finally began to turn in March '73 when Bob Greenwood and D.B. surveyed the remainder of Ramsden's Crawl and Far Pinnacle Streamway. This area of the E.P.C. survey is only an explorer's sketch and to our delight we found that the inlet did not turn N.W. but continued the S.W. trend of the Ramsden's tube—straight towards the Crumbles! It ended in a sump and muddy side passage which did not correspond with the explorers' description and it was obvious that the passage had been scoured out recently to expose laminated mud amongst shingle beds. We concluded that when the Happy Wanderers diverted the whole of the Easegill flood waters into the Crumbles, it had passed through Far Pinnacle streamway. This was confirmed when the duo roped down two short pitches to Sausage Junction and noted a great mound of loose shingle in Worm Drive.

The Crumbles.

The same diversion had sealed off all the lower chambers of the Crumbles so the H.W. / U.L.S.A. digging team launched an outflanking attack on a rift in the upper series. Tremendous feats of muscle power by Alf Latham, Jake and Ginge (Eric) Hewson finally sank

Black Rabbit Chimney into Square Cavern in the lower series. The system was then surveyed and several small extensions made, but eventually all digs seemed to require massive shoring or blasting. This was disappointing since a sound and draught connection had been established between Pippikin and the Crumbles and the deepest point of the Crumbles, in a very dangerous choke, was only 20 ft. above the Border Sump in Lancaster. The Crumbles was clearly a bridge between the two giants but with the gates locked at both ends.

The Border Sump—Chapter II.

The spring of 1973 saw several trips to the Border Sump in the hope of making progress under dry conditions or by lowering the water level. Maple Leaf Rift was laddered (60 ft. pitch) to provide a flood safe route into Cellar Passage. One of the more exciting trips through Ramsden's took place in high flood when one mad pair took a deep breath and abseiled down to Sausage Junction. They were fortunate to find Cellar Passage with airspace since it has been observed under 40 ft. of water in extreme conditions.

Initially the last pitch down to Sausage Junction was extremely tricky since the only way was to slide along a tube out over the pitch and then drop down and back under using a rope for aid. This move was irreversible but by knocking off flakes a direct free climb in the water is now possible for thin people.

By September the evil moment could be put off no longer—Pooh must dive the sump, but would he fit through Ramsden's Crawl? Due to an L.D. (Logistical Disaster) Tony White, Pooh, A.E., A.B and D.B. dragged a half full 40 cu. ft. bottle through to the Border Sump. A pessimistic Pooh dived without weights or fins since he expected a tight, short, nasty sump. To his horror he found an enlarging tube in which he progressed by lurching along the roof. After 100 ft. it continued 8 ft. wide and 5 ft. high, so our frustrated hero returned to a cool reception after 3 minutes absence. The porters muttered mutinously but carried out the gear to warm up.

Obviously the sump could not remain open and unexplored so D.B. was delegated to organise quick action—an unusual state for U.L.S.A. A trip was booked for the next weekend and the organiser managed to organise himself out of Lancaster and down Pippikin. Of the huge

*party down Lancaster Hole, Daves Parker and Rusbridge, Bob Green-
wood, Colin Ottway and others transported the fully equipped super-
Pooh to the Border Sump. Beyond the previous limit the roof dropped
and at 130 ft. the passage degenerated into a low silted bedding plane
which became too silly for diving after a further 30 ft. As the key
jammed, however, in Lancaster, another began to turn in Pippikin.*

The Hobbit

*Jeff Morgan and D.B. were at that moment on a Pippikin delad-
dering trip. Whilst about it they went to the Hobbit and established a
strong sound connection with the Mistral in Easegill. This was a great
step towards the long sought bottom entrance to Pippikin which would
save the sporting entrance series from destruction during a serious rescue. Next they visited the upper chamber in an aven near Canyon
Streamway where the H.W. had been attacking a narrow downward
crack with a proved draught and sound connection with the Crumbles.
Well greased by mud, D.B. was forced down the crack for 15 ft. and
squirmed sideways into a roomy but trodden passage, which was found
to be the tunnel below the 12 ft. climb in the Hobbit. Undaunted by
the anticlimax the draught was followed down a revolting muddy passage explored by Chas Yonge's party into a clean-washed area with
grass and bits of debris (including polythene) on the roof. Clearly this
was another consequence of the diversion of Easegill into the Crumbles.
Downstream was unexplored territory. Beyond a narrow aven a way
was bulldozed through shingle to a menacing pool with lowering airspace. Upstream was the clean-washed choke attacked by Chas and Co.
who progressed up 20 ft. and along the same distance. In an obscure
corner beneath a roof of poised breccia was a hole down into a black
space. Careful wriggling proved the hole to be passable into a handsome
passage (The Frontier) floored by blocks and then silt. A short crawl
ended in an active high roof fissure and more comfortable walking
ended in a boulder choke sporting odd giant black marbles and a single
tree root stretching from floor to roof.
The attack was continued the following weekend when a scaling
pole wielded by Andy brought down several tons of roof above the Hobbit to reveal an upper chamber and rifts choked by silt and boulders.
Colin, in the Mistral, could hear the voices of the diggers in the new*

chamber so in an emergency a rapid entrance can be made here. Andy and D.B. surveyed the extension explored the previous weekend, (300ft.) and confirmed the pool to be a sump with an inlet passage, choking off, under The Frontier. The survey confirmed that the very loose choke leading to The Frontier was under the Crumbles as suspected, but a way in through this chaos would be difficult to engineer and unstable.

Connection Proved.

October 27th is crucial in our story. On this day Steve Crabtree and Paul Everett put dye into the sump near the Frontier while Nick Lewis, Colin, Steve Jones, Alan Goulbourne and D.B. made a determined attack on the Border Sump. They lowered it 8 inches to open up the first airbell with a great booming and slurping. A pool in the side passage also drained in sympathy to expose a muddy dig. The dye in Pippikin was rendered superfluous when Paul returned later to the Frontier sump and found it lower by 6 inches or so. The Border and Frontier sumps were in fact one and the same and the connection between Pippikin and Lancaster was proved at last. The last key is the biggest. To force the way through, however, Border Sump will have to be drained by trenching, bailing or pumping but it is merely a question of hard work—and time!

For the next two years I did very little caving. I had some interesting adventures following the hippy trail to Nepal. I did some trekking in the Himalaya. Not so many people were doing it then and I'm glad I saw something of Nepal before huge numbers of westerners started to flock to this ancient kingdom.

I stayed in Nepal until my money was almost exhausted and then made a dash down India by train (third class) to catch a flight from Madras to Perth in West Australia. I had purchased my ticket in a travel agency in Delhi before going to Nepal. I had got the ticket on the cheap using a forged student card. Unfortunately when I arrived in the Air India office in Madras I was informed that my ticket was invalid, as the reduction in fare had been granted on the understanding that I was an Indian student on my way to study in Australia. Being an ex British student clearly didn't count! This was rather a shock and pretending to know nothing whatsoever about the general illegality of my ticket I pleaded that I be allowed on to the flight. I was told that this was not possible as the flight was fully booked and my name was not on the passenger list. Eventually the manager of the office became involved. He was a very friendly gentleman and taking pity on me gave me a confirmed booking on a flight to Perth six weeks in the future.

I managed to survive the six weeks spending most of this period living on a beach and subsisting mainly on rice. This was not a happy time. I was suffering badly from dysentery and living on the beach were several vicious, horribly diseased dogs. I was terrified of being bitten by one and getting rabies or some other dreadful infection. I was most relieved when I was allowed to board the plane. As it headed out over the deep blue Indian Ocean I looked down and realised I was flying over the beach were I had been staying. It looked idyllic from this height.

The Australian economy was booming and I found a job the day after my arrival. I quickly accumulated more money than I had ever possessed and started to think about where to go next. Before leaving England I had been talking to Dave Brook about a trip he and others were planning to New Guinea. I had said that I was interested in this trip should it become reality. I contacted Dave from Australia; the trip was on and I sent him some money to secure my place. After working for a year I had saved enough money to go to New Guinea and do some more travelling. I left my job at an oil refinery and set off to the eastern states of Australia.

I decided I would like to go up the highest mountain in Australia—Mount Kosciusko. There is a road to the top but I wanted to walk up through the bush so decided to set off from the ski area at Thedbo. My bus arrived just before dark and I bivvied out on one of the ski runs. In the morning I set off up the mountain and easily reached the summit. It was nearly the beginning of winter and there was an icy wind and freezing rain. I only had a very inaccurate tourist map of the area and what I should now have done was walk and hitch-hike my way off the mountain on the road. Instead I decided to walk down through the wilderness to rejoin the main road north of Thedbo.

I quickly lost height until I was back to the tree line. Unfortunately by now I had lost the path I had been following. I calculated a rough compass bearing to walk on and set off into the trees. The situation now quickly began to deteriorate. As I lost height the vegetation became thicker and thicker and it was very difficult to make progress through the forest. To add to my problems I kept intersecting steep sided narrow stream valleys that were very difficult to cross. On one occasion the only way I could reach the far side was to swing across—Tarzan like—on the branch of a tree. I had expected to reach a road by dark but I realised that I was going to spend another night out. The afternoon passed in a flash and the rain became torrential. I started to get very cold and realised that my situation was very serious.

When it got dark I got into my sleeping bag and ate an inadequate meal. I did not have much food left. I had no waterproof to cover my sleeping bag and soon it was soaking wet. I slept only for short periods and kept waking up shivering. I got up at first light and packed my rucksack. My sleeping bag was now far too heavy to carry as it was saturated with water. I dumped it along with all none essential items I was carrying. I knew that I had to get out of this wilderness before the evening.

I set off. The general trend of the land in the direction I needed to be in was still downward but my progress was dreadfully slow and I was feeling weak and very cold. It was still raining. At around midday I intersected a much larger stream. This was not as hard to cross as some of the others and it did not matter that the water was more than waist deep as I was soaking wet already. I now had to start going upwards in order to follow the compass bearing I was relying on to get me back to civilisation. Also, the undergrowth seemed to have got thicker. I could make no progress at all.

I sat down to consider my situation. I came to the unpleasant conclusion that I was probably going to die. Nobody knew where I was and my body would probably not be found for years. I would simply disappear. I had arranged to meet my sister in Newcastle, New South Wales, in a few days' time. I could imagine how at first she would be annoyed that I was late. She would then become worried and try to find out what had happened to me. I could imagine the worry and distress I was going to cause to my family and this upset me far more than the prospect of dying young.

For want of anything else to do I ate my remaining food. This made me feel a bit better. Now what? I felt silly just sitting around, but what to do? I was unable to continue in the direction I had been heading and I did not think there was any possibility of reversing the route I had come. Then a possible way out of this mess occurred to me. I walked back to the stream and jumped in.

I hoped that perhaps I would get washed along to somewhere where I could actually make progress out of the forest before something very unpleasant happened. I tried not to think about waterfalls.

The water was very cold but it was good to be making fast progress at last. I almost was having fun. After about twenty minutes to my immense excitement I passed under a man-made object—a small pipe going across the stream. I thrashed my way to the bank, grabbed a branch of a bush and hauled myself out of the water. I walked back to the pipe. The pipe had a small path running alongside it and this I followed. Soon this path joined a forestry track. I set off downwards. I was shivering violently but did not care, I had cracked it! After about half an hour I came upon a hut. Smoke was coming out of the chimney. I knocked on the door and was greeted by a dour looking forester. "Who the hell are you?" he grunted.

I explained that I had experienced a bit of a problem walking down from Mount Kosciusko and had lost the path. Please, was there any chance of me drying off my clothing and perhaps having a bite to eat?

"What path? Never heard of any path! Come in, you stupid pom. When my mate gets back we're going in to town. We'll give you a lift if you like." An hour later, fed and dry, I was heading down the track in the back of a truck. It had finally stopped raining and the clouds lifted. I saw the top of Mount Kosciusko. It looked a very long way away and I had a great view of the dense forest I had fought my way through. Yes, I was indeed a very stupid pom.

As it turned out the start of the New Guinea Expedition was delayed so I decided to go back to the UK for a while.

Bob Churcher is not like your average caver. He was, until retirement, an army officer and looks and sounds the part. Geoff Yeadon and Bear used to have fun trying to take off some off his better statements:
"Plucky little bird," or
"Time to let off the nukes old chap!" or
"Tough, damned tough!"
Bob was to coin a phrase "Hard, damned hard" and did some awesome cave diving in the 'seventies. In my opinion, his best efforts were pushing the very far reaches of Little Neath River Cave in South Wales and some pioneering work in Dub Cote in Yorkshire. What made his exploits even more outstanding is the fact that Bob is 'Large, damned large!'
While I was in England waiting to depart on the New Guinea '75 expedition, I was lucky enough to do some very excellent caving, diving and partying with Bob. I'm sure the sort of parties we were going to would have shocked the members of the regimental officers' mess and all I will mention now is that my behaviour at one of these carry-ons enabled Bob to blackmail me for lots of beer for years to come. I did not want even cavers to know (still don't for that matter!). This period culminated in a brilliant week I had in the Dales with Bob, Tony Boycott, and Tessa Pierce. Without much planning we managed to make

one major Three Counties link and almost make a further two break-throughs in Pippikin. It amuses me now to read my caving log from this carefree week:

<u>*Monday: Gavel Pot*</u>

I didn't go down as I was ill. Bob was to dive downstream but went upstream by mistake. He went as far as the deep pot.

<u>*Tuesday: Juniper Gulf*</u>

A festerous trip on SRT. Bob and I made it to the bottom. We then went to the Helwith Bridge and got as pissed as arseholes.

<u>*Thursday: Rift Pot*</u>

After a festerous day open water diving in the Lake District and a night of only moderate drinking we managed to get it together to find Rift Pot and get down to the bottom of the big pitch. Terry Whitaker was on this trip. Terry, Bob and myself went to the sump and got the line belayed. I then went back to the bottom of the big pitch and set off with the remaining gear on my own—leaving instructions for nobody to go into the sump passage due to the possibility of a flash flood. After much knitting I kitted up and dived the vile sump for 30 m. It was horrible and to go further would have been silly. I then crawled the 300m back to the big pitch fully kitted. We then went out reasonably quickly, making the Helwith Bridge in good time. A good trip.

<u>*Friday: Tatham Wife Hole*</u>

On this trip Bob, Tony, Tessa and myself tried to push North West Passage but failed.

<u>*Saturday: Pippikin Pot*</u>

After a Hill Inn disco and a night of hardly any sleep at Widdle Head Barn, this trip would have in most cases been cancelled; but due to the publicity this diving trip had received, it had to be done.

We couldn't have done it without two guys we met in the Hill (J Fox and J L Preston). The conversation went like this.

"Are you Dave Yeandle?"

"Afraid so."

"Can we come on your trip down Pippikin tomorrow? We'll ladder it up for you."

"Thanks, we were a bit worried about laddering as we have no ladders."

In the morning I managed to scrounge a line reel off Bob and eventually we got going. The party consisted of the two guys we met in the pub, Tessa, Tony and myself.

I think our two new friends (J Fox and J L Preston) were a bit disappointed by the disorganised nature of the venture they had so kindly become part of. In any case they set off to Leck Fell ahead of us to start laddering up the tight entrance series. Bob would have nothing to do with this trip, knowing how small parts of Pippikin were and how large he was compared to the rest of us.

Tessa, Tony and myself staggered down Leck Fell to the entrance, laden with diving gear, wondering how on earth we were going to manage it all underground. We were very pleased to find our new friends at the entrance who informed us that they had teamed up with two other cavers. They did not know who they were but they had volunteered to help. These new people had gone on ahead into the cave and were laddering it up. So now we had five of us to carry the diving gear and the ladders for the lower pitches. This trip seemed to be just happening on it's own. All I had done was say I was going to dive both sumps at the end of Pip. People were so willing to help me that it was now actually getting done.

We just seemed to zip down the cave and the diving gear was not a problem. I suppose we were young, fit and on form. It was all going rather well. At the junction with Ratbag Inlet we caught up with our new members and made our introductions.

"Pleased to meet you, Pooh. I'm Dave Savage."

I was astonished. "Not the Dave Savage who pushed Wookey Hole!"

"Well yes, I haven't done much caving for a while; I fancied a look at Pippikin but we didn't bring enough ladders. It was lucky for us we met up with your party."

I was getting even more amazed now. Here was the guy who along with Mike Wooding had been first to Swildon's 12. He had been one of my schoolboy heroes. Now he was helping me to do a dive and he seemed to be nearly as disorganised as I was, and a really nice bloke. Upon reaching the final pitch we discovered that we were still short of one ladder. Dave Savage was still above the previous pitch and agreed to stay where he was and lower a ladder from that pitch, to us, to enable us to reach the dive sites.

I decided to dive downstream first. The sump was tight and wide and, becoming disorientated, I did a U-turn and started to swim back the way I had come. I surfaced one metre away from where I had entered the sump. I did not know this though as my friends upon seeing that I was coming back had hidden and turned out their lights. My light was a bit dim and I did not realise what was going on. Even so I could hardly believe that I had broken through so easily so I tentatively called out, "Can anybody hear me?" After the inevitable merriment at my expense I dived again and found the way on into an apparently large underwater passage which I followed in poor visibility for about 100m. I turned back before reaching the third margin in my 40 cubic foot bottle, in order that I would have sufficient air for a dive in the upstream sump.

The summer had been dry and water levels in Pippikin were low. This helped with my second dive of the day as the upstream sump started much further along the inlet passage than it had back in 1970 when I had been exploring this part of Pippikin. When it did sump, it did so decisively and I easily followed a small but comfortable sump, in good visibility. I passed two airbells in mounting excitement and reached a slight upward constriction, about 50m from where the sump had begun. I had now almost reached the third margin of a bottle that had been well depleted on the previous dive. A desire for self-preservation now started to dampen my urge to continue. I felt very strongly that I was about to break through into something big and yet I knew I would be taking a big risk going into what may turn out to be an underwater squeeze, with a low air supply. My explorations were usually like this, an almost schizophrenic battle between two personalities, one needing comfort, safety and an easy life; the other needing massive adrenaline hits, success and adventure. Pooh 1 won this little battle and I turned back. Maybe I chose to live, but this possibility was not to prevent Pooh 2, a few years later, being very pissed off indeed at not having discovering Link Pot.

I returned to base, I think in retrospect, near hypothermic but then feeling weak and despondent at having turned back. I gave an account of my dive to my excellent supporters. Tessa gave me some of her food and a hug and we set off out; everybody but myself well pleased with our efforts. We made a short side trip on the way leaving the narrow streamway and climbing up into the spacious Hall of the Ten. This is the place where my mates from the Happy Wanderers had realised that they had hit the jackpot with Pippikin Pot. While resting, I told my newer friends some stories about the Wanderers and my adventures with them, both underground and on the surface—in the Dales, in Europe and in Asia. As I spoke it dawned on me that I loved this crazy game called caving and that I was soon to combine this with my passion for world travel. In a few days time I was finally leaving for New Guinea as an expedition member. I now felt not so bad for having turned back in the sump. New adventures beckoned.

Back in the pub Bob announced that the following day he would like to have another dive in Gavel Pot—this time downstream as he had planned to do earlier in the week. I said I would help him with the carry in and our two supporters from the Hill Inn also gladly volunteered their support.

In the mid 1970s several of us were experimenting with Single Rope Technique (SRT) which was then relatively new to British cavers. A few weeks back I had abseiled down Gaping Gill main shaft with Andy Eavis and we had tandemed up on the same rope—Andy a few metres above me and taking photos of me as I went. I didn't have a clue how to SRT properly and was just making it up as I went along. We decided that the best way to dive Gavel downstream sump was for all four of us to go to the top of the final pitch on ladders and then Bob and myself descend to the sump on SRT and have the other guys lower the gear down to us. This all worked out great with Bob and myself descending the final pitch competitively fast, making loud silly noises. We didn't bother about where the rope hung or anything like re-belays, deviations or whatever; as all that had yet to be invented. Our 'techniques' were not destined to make it into any future SRT manuals.

This time I pointed Bob the right way and he entered the downstream sump. He was diving on twin 50 cubic foot bottles. Even so I started to get alarmed when he still was not back after what seemed a very long time. (I did not have a watch). Eventually I reached the dreadful conclusion that Bob had either broken through to airspace or had run out of air and was dead. All I could do for the time being was keep on waiting and I was immensely relieved when I detected movement on the line, shortly followed by that most welcome of sights, the lights of a returning cave diver.

Bob burst out of the sump and announced in his booming voice: "Dave, I have been to Ireby Fell!"

"No you haven't, Bob. Ireby is upstream, not downstream, and a few miles away."

"Well I'm damned if I know where I have been then. I came across a line, followed it and surfaced in this large streamway. It's obviously Ireby Fell!"

"Bob, how far did you swim?" I asked, having trouble taking this conversation too seriously.

"About 600 feet, jolly fine sump." We went on in this vein for a while. It was clear that Bob had connected Gavel to Lost John's. This was a major Three Counties link and the silly bugger still insisted that he had been to Ireby Fell Cavern. I suspected Ireby was one of the few caves in the area he actually knew the name of. I was very glad this excellent nutter hadn't drowned on me.

That evening Bob had to return to the officers' mess and probably, soon after, some horrible war zone. He dropped me off at a good hitch-hiking spot. I forget where to.

The years roll by: Caving for months on end in the jungles of New Guinea and seeing what was the end of a Stone Age culture. Then Australia again, living amongst the ruins of tropical city Darwin in the aftermath of cyclone Tracy. Riding my 500 cc Yamaha through the outback of the Kimberlies on gravel roads and onwards south to Perth, as fast as I could with dwindling money. Then getting a job with a mining company and turning the bike around, heading back north to the Pilbara, to a barren life in a barren land—but with lots of money. Two years of this, then I quit my job and on to Thailand, Hill tribes and the Golden Triangle. Then back to England to rediscover caving. Within a month, over to France and once again to the Pierre Saint Martin. Then a move back to Leeds.

Living in Leeds again was fun and I soon was doing some great caving and cave diving with Geoff Yeadon, Bob (Henpot) Emmett, and the NCC. King Pot was still 'going' and I became part of its exploration. I had been out of England during a very exciting time for cave divers and one night in the pub Geoff asked me if I regretted having missed out.

"No Geoff," I replied. "I wanted to see the world while it was still worth seeing."

"Sounds like farting about to me," retorted Geoff with a grin.

Geoff, however, had not been farting about. He and Bear had become brilliant, world class, cave divers. In Britain no one came close to their achievements. Step by step they had pushed the limits in Kingsdale and by now had connected the down stream sump in Kingsdale Master Cave to the resurgence at Keld Head.

I think I first met Lindsay Dodd in the summer of '75, on the A 65 trunk road. He was walking backwards from Leeds to Kendal to raise money for the New Guinea '75 expedition; and as a result of this effort he was in the Guinness Book of Records for a number of years. At that time he had recently dropped out of a food science course at Leeds

University and was working with Sid Perou making caving films. He was one of Sid's longer-term assistants, was doing the sound recording and also helping to organise Sid's operations.

After my return from overseas in 1978, Lindsay and I caved together a bit and drank together quite a lot. By this time he had secured a job as an assistant sound recordist at Yorkshire Television and was starting to metamorphose from wild dropout student to flamboyant media personality.

Lindsay and Geoff wanted to make a film for television recording the first through dive from Kingsdale Master Cave to Keld Head. With Lindsay's expertise and growing contacts within the media this vision became reality. Many cavers and divers seemed to get sucked into the vortex of 'The Keld Head Film' and I was one. The part I played was small but I'm glad I was involved in this sometimes hilarious, but often manic, over-the-top venture.

The winter of '78/'79 was one of the most severe in a hundred years. My most vivid memory of the Keld Head Film is driving Lindsay from the Dales to Leeds, via Bob Makin's lab at Lancaster University. There was a serious blizzard on the go and Lindsay was in a hurry to make some deadline or other. The roads were almost deserted and the windscreen wipers on my car couldn't cope with all the snow falling out of the pitch-black sky. I drove as fast as I dared with the car stereo full on playing *War of the Worlds*. Lindsay, when he wasn't taking the piss out of my driving, insisted on singing along with the music, loudly and very out of tune.

I also remember being cold a lot of the time. Late one night we were all waiting for Geoff to emerge from Keld Head after a preliminary dive. It was a beautiful crystal clear night with a full moon and countless stars. The deep snow was frozen solid and long icicles decorated the small limestone outcrop over the resurgence. We had already missed the pub and were cold and hungry. I started to jump up and down to try to keep warm. This didn't seem to work so I started to move my arms about and kick high into the air. Helen Herbage declared that I must have learnt this 'dancing' from a primitive tribe in some jungle. This comment caused some merriment and pretty soon we were all leaping up and down and making silly noises. We must have looked a bit mad but it cheered us up a little.

During the period we were involved with filming in Kingsdale. Exciting discoveries were being made by the Northern Pennine Club over in Easegill. They had dug open a shaft in Easegill Beck and dropped into a large passage which they rapidly explored to the top of Echo Aven in Lancaster Hole. Meanwhile other passages in this new cave they had named Link Pot were being discovered and some of these were heading towards Pippikin Pot.

Andy Eavis had a few years previously climbed Echo Aven and if at the top he had only entered a hole over the other side he would have found Link Pot. Not wanting to miss out in a similar manner, I felt I should return to Waterfall Chamber in Pippikin and do another dive in the upstream sump. This dive kept on getting delayed—partly because I was busy with the filming and partly because I had trouble getting enough helpers. I knew I had probably left it too late when I heard that Bob Hryndyj had dived at the end of a passage called Easy Street in Link Pot and got through to an underwater passage which sounded from his description to be the same place I had been in 1975.

One Saturday morning, shortly after hearing about this imminent connection between Pippikin and Lancaster/Easegill/Link, Geoff and I were in our sleeping bags at Henpot's caravan. Once again Henpot had given us accommodation after a night in the Craven Heifer pub. I was not feeling well and things got even worse for me when Bob Hryndyj unexpectedly burst into the caravan and said to the already arisen Henpot, "Hey, Henpot, can you lend me a line reel? I need it to clinch the connection from Link to Pippikin before Pooh has a chance to do it the other way, upstream from Pippikin!" He then noticed to his surprise that the very same Pooh was glaring at him from a horizontal position in a sleeping bag. Somewhat embarrassed at this discovery Bob for once was lost for words. Unlike me, Henpot was most amused and laughing too much to reply to Bob's request. I could hear quiet chuckling coming from the direction of the Yeadon pit. "Go on, let him take it, Henpot," I said in ill humour. "I'll get my revenge on you Hryndyj," I added in frustration. "Now get out of here and leave me to die in peace," I concluded illogically in reference to my unmanageable hangover.

Bob made the connection that day and I never did "get my revenge." A few years later Geoff pushed the downstream sump in Pippikin—the one I had dived immediately prior to doing the upstream sump. He broke through to dry passage and named it "Pooh's Revenge."

The Underground Eiger by Lindsay Dodd

Leeds, February 21, 1979: In a crowded bar the closing credits of *The Underground Eiger* dissolve into the commercials and the *Ten o' clock News*. The audience modestly applaud; almost all had been involved in the television programme. Keld Head, July 6, 1978: Five years of work, 1.8 kilometres of diving line—Geoff Yeadon and Oliver (Bear) Statham link the downstream sump in the West Kingsdale system to its resurgence at Keld Head. Only the satisfaction of the through-dive remains.

Leeds, September 29, 1978: An idea on paper. A busy executive rushing for a train listens patiently for ten minutes, takes the paper and catches the train.

Leeds, October 3, 1978: The bait has been taken; a television company hooked by the line 'Dead Man's Handshake.'

Leeds, October 9, 1978: A desk, a phone, a producer, a film crew, an expense account, a deadline, a headache!

Plied with booze on a Yorkshire Television expense-account lunch, Geoff Yeadon told producer Barry Cockcroft the story of Keld Head. For Ian Plant, local newspaperman and cave diver, the tension was too great and he collapsed with hysterics in the washroom. Bear was on holiday abroad, unaware that a television company was interested in making a feature documentary on the through-dive.

Later that afternoon, still heady from the lunch, I met Bob Makin, electronics wizard at Lancaster University. I asked him: "Could a diver talk to the surface using your speleophone system as he swam through Keld Head?" Bob, an eternal optimist, said he could. He had already perfected his cave-to-surface speleophone system; now all he had to do was make it work underwater!

Thus the show got on the road; the last documentary to be filmed in Yorkshire Television's six-part series titled *Once in a Lifetime* and known at this stage as Program 6400—Cave Diving.

The star double act were quickly signed up: Mostafa Hammuri and Bob Emmett. Musty and Henpot. Musty, a Jordanian, and a charming epitome of all you ever imagined a film cameraman to be: fast car, immaculate dresser with expensive tastes. Mostafa first got hooked on Keld Head when he saw a photograph of Geoff in his gear. Cave diving, Musty decided from then on, was for him.

With a *carte blanche* from YTV he was a salesman's dream come true and in a twin-set back pack with spare valve, tailor-made wetsuit (ready-made ones being the wrong colour), and space-age helmet and light, he certainly looked the part. Pity someone hadn't taught him how to dive!

Henpot, local cave diver, dressed with sartorial elegance in clogs, tarpaulins and souwester, drives a battered van, is a frustrated professor of farmyard physics and spends his spare time making snow tractors. He is employed by YTV as driver, diver extraordinaire, odd-job man, entertainer and chief dog-handler. Musty was so horrified by Henpot's wardrobe he kept giving him his spare clothes.

Very soon the technology became awe-inspiring. Miniature 16-millimetre film cameras fitted with semi-fish-eye lenses to compensate for bad visibility were developed and placed in underwater housings to film the through-trip. Ultrasonic diver-to-diver communication devices were purchased; microphones were tested in a compression chamber, and underwater housings commissioned for miniature tape recorders. Anticipating the yet-unfinished underwater speleophone we investigated underwater speech and replaced the standard diver's mouthpiece with a 'wetmask,' providing the necessary airspace to formulate words. The wetmask was crammed with microphones to link with the speleophone, the ultrasonic gear, and the tape recorder. To enable the diver to speak continuously throughout the dive one wetmask had to be worn at all times, and had to be capable of being supplied by any of the three bottles. The 110-cubic-foot, 3,000-p.s.i. bottles had an octopus rig fitted on the first stage allowing each bottle to be fitted with a demand valve and a special snap-link connector permitting any bottle to be used to supply the valve connected to the wetmask. Each diver had, therefore, three bottles and four demand valves.

Lighting was expected to be a critical problem as visibility was known to be about three metres at best, making commercially available underwater lights (where the lamp is attached to the camera) of limited use due to excessive back scatter. Back scatter, the reflection of light by small particles in the water, was avoided by designing a lighting set-up where batteries were strapped to the divers' bottles. Each neutrally buoyant battery pack would supply 250 watts of light for 50 minutes at a cost of £500. One diver could carry two packs. Bear was to film and Geoff do the lighting.

Towards the end of October, Bear was firmly entrenched in the chaos, Bob Makin was working overtime encapsulating his precious electronics in a length of drainpipe whilst I wrestled with the technology and storyline.

Barry Cockcroft has achieved a reputation for making human documentaries, therefore one of the key objectives of this film was to explore the characters of Geoff and Bear. The film was conceived to be in two parts—conveniently separated by a commercial break. The first would give the background and history and establish the unique personalities involved. The second part would be the day of the dive. We intended to use archive 8-millimetre film shot in 1950 by Reg

Hainsworth of the first-ever free dive in Keld Head, to film Geoff and Bear at work in their pottery, to tell of their involvement with Keld Head and also to include what was to prove to be a controversial sequence of a booze-up in the Hill Inn. Compared to the purist approach of depicting cave development in West Kingsdale, and its exploration by abseiling down Rowten and following the course of the water to the downstream sump, cynics may say we took the easy way out.

It was now November and the schedules dictated that the film should be transmitted in January. The pressures were increasing. December 13 was pencilled in for the date of the through-dive. The filming commenced with three days of tests at Keld Head. Fortunately, the resurgence is only a few metres from a road, making logistics simple. Unfortunately, Mostafa insisted on filming underwater at Keld Head. It took him at least four hours to get into the water; then he had epic troubles with his equipment, needed four times as much compressed air (he called it "hoxygen") as anyone else, and needed another diver (Bob Hyrindij) to carry his huge conventional camera and lights underwater.

The hurriedly assembled miniature cameras, lights and tape recorder housings began to arrive. Despite costing over £5,000 the manufacturing defects were immense: the neutrally buoyant battery lamps sank; the cameras had more design faults than a plastic carbide lamp, relying totally on an elastic band for their operation; the underwater housings for the tape recorders leaked.

Barry Cockcroft, a veteran non-worrier, seemed more than a little pensive. We had four weeks to complete the shooting.

Bob Makin's speleophone was far from completion. What may appear to an outsider as a major technological advance is really a good idea, made practical through a series of innovations. It was these that were at the heart of the machine's progress: the connectors, that crucial component, that special electronic device—the list is endless. The importance of each individual part is minimal compared with the result achieved through their inspired combination. Their assembly was time-consuming and was the frustrating limiting factor in the production of the device. Bob was to spend two months on the project, working late into the night.

On November 27 we started to shoot in Skipton, filming Geoff and Bear's lifestyles—Geoff living in his battered Morris 1000 van, and Bear living with his girlfriend, Anne Poole. All good stuff, not too difficult to film. Within the week we were back at Keld Head. To work there we set up a caravan with location catering facilities and had a nine-man film crew, and a support team of up to 17 cavers. Three things were essential for filming underwater at Keld Head: good visibility, good equipment and competent cave divers. We filmed in winter, the frosty weather restricting the level of peat in the water. We eventually got the camera and lights working properly, thanks to Henpot's farmyard technology. We also had Mostafa.

To accomplish the through-dive safely Geoff and Bear would each have to dump a spare bottle 900 metres in, in the middle of the passage. We decided to mock this up near the entrance to Keld Head. With a rope around his waist, Musty went 15 metres into the sump and filmed the event. Whatever you say about Musty you have to admire his guts.

The next day, however, Musty dropped a bombshell. It had to appear in the final film that he had swum the entire 1,830 metres of the cave alongside Geoff and Bear, filming the action. This meant mocking up everything 15 metres inside Keld Head! Tempers flared and principles were outraged, but eventually he was persuaded to accept the silliness of his idea. Half a day of precious filming time had been lost.

Money creates, corrupts, compromises and destroys. We experienced all these qualities in the film's production.

Primarily, the money meant that there were enough resources to finance the technology behind the film; also, special (expensive) sequences were possible—helicopter shots for example. The money also meant that there was a deadline for transmission and whilst giving a sense of urgency, the ever-decreasing time limit did compromise ideals. Also, paying people for their participation can corrupt motivation and destroy their natural enthusiasm. Yet, in a brief respite from a hectic drive, Geoff and I were refreshed in a rather expensive restaurant. As I was about to pay the bill, I was taken by a sudden sneezing fit and blew my nose…on a £10 note. Of course, it was YTV money—it's called hospitality.

Filming resumed. Musty and the rest of the film crew were despatched to London to film Bear's father (the British Ambassador to Brazil) and a small caving team continued experimenting with the miniature cameras, gathering some remarkable footage.

The weather was icy cold. It was no joke spending six hours in the water, but it made for good visibility. As more sequences were gathered it became obvious that there was no way we could contemplate the through-dive on December 13. All the equipment had not been perfected and time was running out.

The crew returned from London and we prepared to film the pub scene. When word got around that YTV were to film at the Hill Inn all the Ingleton rats crawled out of their holes for their pint or two of 'hospitality.' Taking the camera into a room full of carousing cavers was like charging into battle. Beer was thrown directly at the lens and I spent most of the evening wrestling with one bloke who was intent on saying "Hello, mum!" in front of the camera and then exposing himself. The action was mediaeval. I had to hide the petrol from one girl who still regrets not being allowed to perform her fire-throwing act in the crowded pub. Most people involved in the filming are now banned, but Barry and Musty escaped before the debacle ended and the landlord threw everyone out.

Interviews in Bernard's cafe the next day and helicopter shots in Kingsdale terminated the filming before Christmas. Geoff and I returned to Leeds in time for an end-of-term fancy dress party at YTV headquarters. Geoff went dressed normally, but unfortunately passed out and the security men took television's latest star to be a smelly tramp. Fortunately, Geoff was rescued just as they were about to call the police.

Over Christmas a branch of Independent Television went on strike, blacking the screens, but Geoff and I spent the week in a swimming pool modifying equipment and trying to talk to each other using Bob's recently completed speleophone. After saying "Can you hear me?" a thousand times without reply we decided that the pump noise in the pool was interfering with Bob's system.

Wires were sewn into Geoff's drysuit, microphones glued into his mask and, despite warnings that we'd never make it to Kingsdale given the blizzard conditions, Bob Makin, his mate J.C., Geoff and I made it to Keld Head on New Year's Eve. Despite the Arctic conditions it only took an hour to persuade Geoff to get out of the car, and eventually, dressed in his drysuit with the speleophone strapped to his bottles and the snow swirling, he slipped into Keld Head.

Twenty minutes later it was magic…Geoff was 240 metres into Keld Head singing Christmas carols and for once we on the surface were colder than he was, but joining in the choruses. Using tone bleeps and taking cross bearings, we were able to pinpoint his position in the white-out. At last Geoff emerged and proceeded to freeze into his gear. We struggled to extricate him before he became permanently trapped in his drysuit. We had successfully achieved the first-ever two-way wireless contact with an underwater sump-bound diver. Later as we drove to the pub, a comet blazed across the sky—what an omen—and we hadn't touched a drop all day.

YTV was back at work, the strike having given us some breathing space—the program could now be transmitted as late as March. However, January 8 was set for the through-dive. The cold weather continued until the sixth when a warm front passed melting weeks of snow on the hills, causing the worst flood in years. A metre-high mushroom of water rose out of Keld Head, already two metres above normal levels, completely submerging, then removing a water-level indicator concreted there by Lancaster University. The following week, though, frosty weather had returned and the plan for the through-dive sprang into action.

Sunday, January 14, 1979: the extra bottles are dumped in Keld Head; both Geoff and Bear have leaks in their high pressure systems—perhaps due to the 4,500 p.s.i. of compressed air in bottles rated at 3,000 p.s.i. The bottles are dumped just short of Dead Man's Handshake, 900 metres in. Geoff, wearing the speleophone and tape recorder, goes through the infamous constriction in 18 metres of water to check it isn't blocked and locates its position on the surface 150 metres above.

Monday, January 15, 1979: The day before the dive; cameras and tape recorders are checked, batteries charged. Up and down Kingsdale 200 flashing lights staked at nine-metre intervals mark the route of the dive. The day draws to a close and a select few gather for a meal. YTV hospitality' means that no one is completely sober that night and what with last-minute checks and the booze it is late before we crash out.

Tuesday, January 16, 5.00 a.m.: Refreshed after four hours sleep we wake, singing with undertones of outrageous black humour.

7.00 a.m.: Two film crews arrive for breakfast, but when we are about to depart Geoff is nowhere to be seen. Mostafa is there; having been recently forced to sell his fast car he arrives in a Mini. Suddenly Geoff appears in a chauffeur-driven Lambourgini Espada. Musty is in the process of declaring the car "rubbish" when a crash rends the air. The wall he's parked in front of suddenly collapses, sending boulders crashing onto his Mini. One up over Musty at last.

8.00 a.m.: An exhilarating drive to Kingsdale in the Lambourgini (with instructions not to touch the upholstery) where we meet the 'dogs.' We film them carrying gear underground.

10.30 a.m.: Geoff and Bear arrive at the sump and begin kitting up. The cameras are loaded and we keep in touch with the surface using the speleophone. One hundred metres above us Anne Poole, Bob

Makin and J.C. prepare to follow the course of the dive and two film crews get into position to cover their progress.

12.30 pm.: Geoff: "I lie on my back in 15 centimetres of water, mummified in 73 kilograms of diving gear. I check each piece of equipment, hampered by the well-meaning chaos of helpers. Four 'dogs' lift me to my feet and help me stagger, breathless, like a beached whale, to deeper water."

Both divers are kitted up, Bear has the cameras, Geoff the lights and speleophone. Each diver carries a small tape recorder loaded with three hours of tape to talk his way through Keld Head.

"...Bear makes final checks and disappears into the sump. I sink into the water and at last become weightless in the murk.

"Suddenly, Bear returns. The strap on his helmet has broken. A quick repair and he disappears once more. He is taking the lead as he has not explored the first 800 metres of the tunnel and can use the good visibility to make the journey easier.

"I adjust my buoyancy, turn to wave goodbye to the security of 20 lights and disappear through the foam into a vat of Guinness-coloured water: the downstream sump in Kingsdale."

12.45 p.m.: Geoff sets off on the through-dive leaving a score of helpers staring at the sump.

"At last we are on our way, each breath of dry air a reminder of the trust I place in the tangle of tubes and valves now writhing in the murk. Whatever happens, we are on our own. We have agreed that if one of us has to turn back the other will help him out and not go on alone.

"Suddenly, Bob Makin's voice crackles through my ear piece and reminds me that I'm on TV.

"I follow Bear down a steep gravel slope. I cannot see him; only the rhythmic flurry of silt, disturbed by his fins, shows me where he has been. I can talk to the surface 120 metres above, but for most of our journey all I will see of Bear will be the tips of his fins. We have no vocal link between us.

"As I glide through the tea-coloured water, never leaving the security of the diving line, I occasionally bump into rock, but rarely see the passage. I am encased in a gloom without walls.

"Over the first 400 metres I rely on my memory of the exploration. This is the worst part of the dive—the roof is very low and the silt at its thickest. I can see almost nothing. All the time Bob Makin speaks, and I answer by transmitting tone. It is an unreal situation.

"Two hundred and ten metres in, I reach a constriction in the passage where I have to feed my huge cylinders and speleophone through. All non-essential gear can be dumped, and with my head one-quarter buried in silt Bob continues to talk whilst I struggle. Sci-fi becomes fact! I'm in an extremely difficult situation six metres underwater and yet all the time a relaxed voice calls me from the surface.

"Three hundred metres in, the passage is larger. Bear has the camera, a television reporter whom I've never met calls down the speleophone, 'We feel for you down there, Geoff.' I don't believe it and nearly drown while laughing. Anne Poole takes over and I tell her not to ring me when she knows I'm too busy to answer.

"Six hundred metres in, I'm looking directly into Bear's eyes. He looks annoyed at me for exploring such a small passage, but there's only 1,200 metres to go and the worst is over. I take the lead. Six hundred and seventy metres in I reach the edge of a 15-metre shaft and wait for Bear. I look for the expression on his face. Snap, identical to mine on my first trip. His Adam's Apple goes up and down and his pupils flicker as he examines the advancing gaping hole. Carefully, we descend into the shaft, visibility is better here and we see the walls towering above us. One of the most impressive moments of any trip; our depth gauges wind up as the walls disappear again at the foot of the shaft 19 metres underwater. The passage is huge—definitely the way to Keld Head.

"We continue and soon reach the point where we made the connection. I recall how remote it felt from the Keld Head end.

"Nine hundred metres in the passage narrows—this is the beginning of Dead Man's Handshake (I barely think of the time when I thought I'd held Jochen Hassenmayer's hand for the last time when he was trapped, lost in this constricted maze). The filming lights go on again to capture this moment and as I burst through the final squeeze the passage seems just too big. The lights let us see for 10 metres, but this is not enough to see the full width of the passage.

"Thirty metres farther in we bump into our reserve air supply, dumped two days ago from Keld Head. We help each other on with the backpacks and get a majestic boost of confidence. With nearly 900 metres still to go I feel as though I am out. The relief is tremendous, I press the button, 'Show me the way to go home' I sing into the speleophone. The passage seems like the road home from work on a foggy day.

"Eventually, 45 metres from the rising, YTV silliness overtakes us. Musty cannot get himself together to film our emergence and we have to wait 15 minutes for him to set up his camera at Keld Head. Finally, Bob says we can come out.

"My only memory of surfacing is having too many people to face and at the same time having an enormous bogie on the end of my nose."

3.00 p.m.: Geoff and Bear emerge in the resurgence pool to be greeted by Anne Poole spewing champagne, and Mostafa filming , both up to their waists in water, surrounded by a strangely silent crowd. Perhaps in the cold drizzle of the afternoon they had become bored. We corrected this using a sound effect in the studio. A few hours later we all proceeded to get outrageously drunk in the Craven Heifer.

Reluctantly, the next day we staggered, bleary-eyed, underground once more to obtain extra footage of the carry to the sump. We were, however, revived by coffee heavily laced with brandy, and by the spectacle of the lady production assistant re-applying her make-up after going through the entrance duck.

On our return to Leeds a few days later the hierarchy of Independent Television offered a 50-minute, prime time, fully networked slot (what jargon!), if we could edit the material in three and a half weeks. This was the hardest stage of the production. Up to 16 hours every day were spent immersed in the film, seeing some sequences more than 200 times. Eventually we had three editors working full-time to meet the deadline.

We also needed one extra day of shooting. Because of the misty conditions on the day, we couldn't get the planned helicopter shots of the surface team switching on the lights in Kingsdale, and we had planned for the closing shot in the film a 1,830-metre track along the lights from the helicopter, shot at dusk.

We staked out the lights, had the chopper in the air, but owing to an exposure cock-up nothing registered on film. Disappointing—but that's all in the game; there wasn't time to re-shoot.

Eventually, in a mad rush we completed the editing just in time and at 9 p.m. on Wednesday, February 21, *The Underground Eiger* hit an unsuspecting audience of at least 20 million. Thank Christ it was all over!

A Dog's Life on "The Underground Eiger"
by Simon Garvey & Stuart Herbage (From ULSA Review, #15, August 1979).

Yorkshire Television's film, *The Underground Eiger*, about the world's longest cave dive by Geoff Yeadon and Oliver (Bear) Statham is now probably familiar to most cavers. However, there was much that happened behind the scenes that may not be so well known…

Strangely enough, this adventure started for us in the Pack Horse, Leeds, one Thursday evening when Lindsay Dodd came round desperately trying to recruit helpers for the upcoming YTV production *The*

Underground Eiger. Lucrative offers were made in the form of the extensive use of YTV credit and so, late in December, 1978, 12 broke Leeds cavers set off for the Dales.

Most of us were under the impression that our job would merely be to carry diving and filming equipment into and out of the cave, so it was with some surprise that we found ourselves being filmed getting out of our pits in the Northern Cave Club hut at Braida Garth on the first morning. None of us having been to R.A.D.A. or anywhere near it, we got our first and only acting lessons from the producer Barry Cockcroft (nicknamed variously 'Baz' and Barry Cock-up) which consisted of "act naturally" and "ignore the camera." Both these pieces of advice were difficult to follow in the then smelly and overcrowded hut but, amazingly, this scene took only two hours to film under the glare of TV lights which seemed more suited to a pop concert. Suprisingly, only two retakes were necessary, but neither because Colin Henderson removed his underpants while Helen Herbage was ceremoniously passing around the coffee.

Soon a pecking order developed, with Geoff and Bear being the stars while the rest of us were regarded as, and called, 'dogs.' Dave Yeandle became Chief Dog because he was the only one who knew how to get air out of the diving bottles in a controlled manner; Colin was Chief Underdog (nobody knows why) and the remainder were dogs with a small 'd,' differentiated only into university dogs and polytechnic dogs.

Although there were only a few of us with any experience of cave filming, courtesy of Sid Perou, we were very unimpressed with the speed of operations underground. The slowness seemed mainly due to the cameraman's, Mostafa's "fantastic shot, Barry," Hammuri's filming positions, notably in the oil drum at Valley Entrance. With Musty and an unfortunate soundman as well as air bottles blocking the way, the straightforward entrance became a squeeze of Pippikin-type proportions. Then, of course, someone would breathe out of turn and Musty would want to film it all over again.

Eventually we progressed as far as the duck, where we spent over two freezing-cold hours standing and swimming in the icy water. Lindsay and Musty, tied together by a lifeline, were pulled through the duck so that they could make tracking shots of people as they came through. Everyone was glad when this part was 'in the can,' although Musty quite enjoyed playing in the water, not surprisingly considering he was wearing a total thickness of ten millimetres of neoprene, Damart underwear and a boiler suit. To finish things off, a phone call from Leeds brought the news that the film of Braida Garth had been accidentally exposed and was completely fogged. We had to do it all again.

The next few days were upset by foul weather. Each morning the water level in the Master Cave had to be checked; this meant changing into ice-cold wetsuits every day for a week. Fill-in shots and interviews were all the filming done during this time. On one occasion while Geoff and Bear were dumping spare diving bottles at Keld Head, Musty waded into the water to film them. Suddenly, he was unfooted by strong currents and disappeared beneath the surface holding his priceless camera aloft like Excalibur. Those in wetsuits nearby seemed unmoved by this turn of events, while Bob Emmet and others in dry clothes stripped off and prepared to swim to the rescue. Fortunately for them, Musty managed to reach the shore before too many people caught pneumonia.

After a week of donning wetsuits and postponements of the dive, we were glad of the filming of the party one evening at the Hill Inn. The plan was very simple—get drunk by 8 p.m.; this we duly did, with a 4.30 p.m. start and a YTV kitty behind the bar to help. At first we were left to the serious business of drinking, but then out came the cameras and things went haywire! Geoff went into his Mick Jagger routine, Bear went upside down, J.C. sang until everyone had seen his tonsils and virtually everyone tried to squeeze through the cartwheel. And for those of you contemplating a game of American football in the Hill Inn, don't bother; we were chucked out for our efforts.

The next day we rose at the crack of dawn to film Geoff and Bear kitting up at Kingsdale Master Cave sump. A sick team of dogs once more had to make the journey into cold wetsuits and Valley Entrance carrying large amounts of diving and filming gear. By the end of the day, some dogs had made seven return trips, sometimes with two diving bottles apiece, while others had craftily shared a bottle between two; or, like Barry Cockcroft, had skived completely. Mostafa insisted that we carry an extra cylinder and his large underwater camera to the sump but, of course, once there they were never used. Nevertheless, they provided some amusement; Paddy, one of the Poly dogs, insisted on carrying the cylinder strapped to his back valve-upright on the way out with a friend, against the earnest advice of the Chief Dog and Bob Emmet. We were still huddled together criticising their actions when there was a loud bang and an ear-piercing hiss not unlike that at a fireworks display. Eventually D.Y. and Henpot became calmer as their hysterical laughter subsided and they ran off to rescue the unfortunate Paddy, whom they found lying on his stomach, compressed air trying to blow his head off. His friend was sensibly sheltered some distance away, presumably waiting to catch the pieces. Luckily, Paddy suffered nothing worse than an extensive blow-wave.

Eventually the day for the dive arrived—bright, not breezy, and definitely not warm. Our wetsuits had frozen solid overnight and most people had at least a centimetre of ice in their wellies. Under the brave leadership of the Chief Dog we were up and carrying gear by an astonishing 5 a.m. Three hours later and several dips into the '9F box' (one of the more pleasant aspects of this epic-on-tap coffee loaded with brandy; it's a union rule that cameramen should always have access to refreshments) all the gear and twenty people were at the KMC sump. Dave Yeandle had been appointed as mouthpiece for the underground end of Bob Makin's speleophone but was soon called away as technical assistant to help Geoff and Bear kit up. From above, the sump appeared very colourful, mainly because of Musty who was sheltering, with his camera, under a large golfing umbrella. Simon Garvey was promoted to mouthpiece and sat at the top of the pitch before the sump. From there, however, he couldn't actually see the sump and this caused a fair bit of confusion for those on the surface. Bob Makin was asking for the estimated time of departure of the divers; this request was received at the top of the pitch, shouted down to Lindsay at the sump who said something totally unintelligible, which was then interpreted and sent back to the surface. Bob's worry about the time of the dive was later to become clear. It had been raining for over two hours and, not only was the surface team getting wet, but Kingsdale Beck was rising with the odd iceberg floating by.

Geoff and Bear set off with Bob Makin, Musty and a soundman in hot pursuit over the surface, jumping walls and wading the beck. Last, but not least, a team of wetsuited dogs traipsed after them as their dry clothes had inadvertently been taken to Ingleton.

Two and a half hours later we arrived at Keld Head to find the successful divers waiting before surfacing until Musty had sorted his camera out. He had no time to change into his wetsuit and so had to wade deep into the water to film.

And then the dive was really over. The champagne didn't fizz, but the flood pulse that had helped carry Geoff and Bear through abated. Still the best line was to come:

"How do you feel?"

"Slightly worse than a trout."

4

King Pot

I n the summer of 1978 I returned to England after spending nearly three years working in outback Australia. I had managed to save up a bit of money. Some of it I had already spent wandering around South-East Asia on my way to England. I was planning to stay in the UK for perhaps three months and thought I would fit in a few caving trips during this period, just for old time's sake of course, and nothing very difficult or dangerous. During my travels I had almost convinced myself that I had no desire to do any more hard caving; and as for cave diving, well that was quite out of the question.

Up on Mendip I went into the Hunters' on a Friday evening. As I walked in the door I was greeted by several of my old caving mates shouting, "It's the Boy!" and demands for pints owed from previous years. Roger Dors greeted me as if I had last been in his pub the weekend before. It was good to be back and very soon Chris Batstone of the BEC had offered to accompany me to Swildon's Sump 2 the following day. We had a lot of fun, splashing around the streamway which was in a sportingly wet condition. I decided to stay up at the Belfry that night as I was having such a good time.

While in the Hunters that evening I heard that the NCC had pushed King Pot in Yorkshire to a series of pitches and crawls that led, eventually, to the East Kingsdale Main Drain (or Master Cave!). Getting quite enthusiastic about caving after a few pints, I told everybody that I would descend this new find at the first opportunity. Shortly after making this decision I was delighted to see that Pete and Alison Moody had arrived. They told me all about how Pete was planning to dive a sump in Lionel's Hole the following day. However, they were in need of transport for the venture. I offered to drive them over to Burrington: and well, I could even help carry the gear down the cave! The evening continued in a jovial fashion and then Pete announced that perhaps he didn't really want to dive all that much. Would I like to do the dive instead?

"Definitely not."
"You wouldn't have to carry any of the gear."
"No way, bugger off Moody."
"I'm sure this sump will go, it's nice as well."
"Oh, all right!"

Come Sunday morning, feeling unwell, I was appalled to discover that Pete and Alison were still very enthusiastic about the trip. Very soon, too soon, accompanied by several other cavers, we were forcing our way down a horrible, cold, tight, muddy cave. Mercifully it didn't take very long to reach the sump. As far as I was concerned the one redeeming feature of this cave was it's short length. Lying in a squalid pond being helped to kit up by Pete, I resolved to only go in for a metre or two and then pretend the sump was too tight, if indeed it wasn't anyway, as seemed rather likely.

I entered feet first on a base fed line. Once under water I felt more relaxed and even though the sump was tight I didn't stop as planned, but kept going and passed the sump after six metres. After only a few metres of cave passage I reached another sump and dived again. After going down vertically for three metres the way on was too small to follow. To my surprise I realised I was enjoying all this!

We emerged into bright sunlight in Burrington Combe. A family was having a picnic outside the entrance. I think they were a bit shocked to see us seemingly appear from nowhere. As cavers will, we started to peel off our muddy rags. We had no intention of causing a fuss but I think our antics rather put the picnickers off their lunch as they quickly relocated further up the road. I was having a lot of fun being back with my caving friends and I realised that I was very quickly fitting back into British caving. I now wanted to do some hard trips!

A few days later I went to Yorkshire. I met John (Lugger) Thorpe and Derek Crossland in the Craven Heifer and they kindly agreed to show me their exciting new finds in King Pot.

I really enjoyed the several sporting wet pitches. I was elated to be rediscovering caving and although King Pot is actually quite a strenuous cave I felt quite at home in this newly opened system. The crawls didn't seem too arduous really and the squeezes not ridiculously tight. The loose boulders I didn't like at all. When we popped out at last into the East Kingsdale Main Drain I was a bit disappointed as it was smaller than The West Kingsdale Master Cave. I soon became impressed again when we reached the upstream sump. I really wanted to dive it! The water was very clear and I could see straight down a wide flooded shaft. There was an excellent place to tie off a line and kitting up would be so easy at the spacious sump pool. I immediately started to enthuse about the possibilities of this site. My enthusiasm was met with a cool response from my companions, who informed me that Derek was planning to dive both the upstream and downstream sumps and I would have to wait my turn should I have plans to dive.

Back on the surface I found that Geoff Yeadon was interested in these sumps too and I offered my services as support diver. We both accepted that Derek should have first crack at them. A few NCC stalwarts were prepared to carry for Derek, but not enough for such a hard carry. We were prepared to help the NCC carry the diving gear in order to get involved in the operation. Our motivation was of course far from altruistic and we planned to get involved in the actual diving as soon as we possibly could.

Dave Timmins and Bob (Henpot) Emmet were keen to join Geoff and myself in helping the NCC dive King. This meant that Derek now had enough carriers. The date was set for the dive and we vaguely arranged with Derek and Lugger to meet in the Craven Heifer the night before to discuss our plan of attack.

Nobody from the NCC actually turned up to this so called 'planning meeting.' To make matters worse Geoff, Dave, Henpot and myself drifted into a heavy drinking session. We ended up more or less collapsing into Henpots' ramshackle caravan—to awake Saturday morning feeling very ill indeed.

We found Lugger, Derek and other NCC wandering around Ingleton. They still intended doing the dive but had failed to organise any air supplies! Fortunately, Henpot had two 50 cubic feet bottles available and after a greasy breakfast and several pints of tea in one of the cavers' cafes we set off to King Pot.

I suffered a lot on the way down the cave. We were all carrying heavy and awkward loads through this tortuous system. Dave, Geoff and myself had very severe hangovers and someone complained that the air in the cave smelt of stale beer fumes. Unlike me and in contrast to my continual groaning, Geoff bore it all in silence. Years later he admitted to me that he really suffered on this carry, saying, "King Pot carrying bottles is quite horrible enough, even without a hangover!"

I just could not get myself going into a relaxed flowing rhythm—so essential on long caving trips and I was wasting energy thrashing around. Derek and Lugger, as usual, were caving very powerfully and had great fun pointing out that I only had myself to blame for my pathetic state. I was in a dreadful mess by the time we reached King Henry Hall. I lay around amongst the boulders groaning. Vowing to lead a healthier lifestyle I concentrated on not being sick. The NCC loved this melodramatic performance and in their delight started to throw rocks at me. I thought this so outrageous that I just had to laugh. I immediately felt a bit better, got to my feet, and started to cave properly.

We reached the downstream sump quickly and Derek kitted up. The sump looked very uninviting and intimidating. The walls of the streamway were covered in slimy mud and the water was dark and cloudy with peat. The sump pool was covered in froth. I was glad I wasn't doing this dive.

Upon diving, Derek discovered he was wearing too much weight. Unfortunately this realisation came too late as he had already begun a head first fall. The sump was steeply sloping and Derek tumbled down rapidly gaining depth and bouncing off small ledges as he went. At a depth of 15m he was stopped by a wider ledge. Derek could see the shaft going on down but wisely chose to turn back. He returned to base by pulling hand over hand on the line.

I think most divers would have felt they had had enough excitement for one day after such a frightening experience. Derek, dedicated and determined explorer that he was, wanted to continue with the diving and we helped him walk fully kitted to the upstream sump. He entered with less lead than downstream and had a much happier dive in two-metre visibility.

He found the sump pool to be 8m deep and the way on down a shingle bank to a depth of 11m. A horizontal bedding led after 70m to a large circular passage which started to decrease in depth. Derek, who was wearing only one wetsuit, was by now very cold and turned back to base.

We were very excited when Derek told us of his dive. The end sounded most promising. I was feeling a little hungry and remembered that I had packed a Mars Bar in my ammunition box. I opened up the box and was confused when I couldn't find the Mars Bar. I noticed that the NCC were watching me and that Lugger was grinning. I came to the conclusion that they had pilfered my rations and accused them of this theft! Nobody owned up and I started to get annoyed. I told them that they really should be more organised and buy their own food. Lugger responded by pushing me into the sump.

We decided to leave most of the gear in the cave to be used for future dives. We stored this equipment on a ledge high above the stream, as a precaution against flooding. We were well pleased with our efforts and made a rapid and enjoyable exit from the cave. There was much hilarious banter as we raced against one another all trying to be first back to the surface with everybody attempting to get away with carrying as little as possible of the remaining diving equipment.

It seemed likely that the King Pot sumps would turn out to be long dives and so we unanimously decided that Geoff should dive next, wearing his dry suit. This meant that we would have extra gear to carry in. However, interest in these sumps was growing and we had no trouble getting extra people to join our team.

The following Sunday the original team, along with many others, assembled at Braida Garth. Most of us had spent Saturday night at a disco in Ingleton and we weren't all in prime shape. I had somehow managed to strain a muscle in my leg while attempting to dance to the Stranglers. I had a bit of trouble walking to the entrance. Once underground I was okay as King Pot is mostly crawling. A fresh cylinder and Geoff's diving gear were taken down very quickly due to the large number of people available to carry.

At the downstream sump Geoff kitted up very smoothly and disappeared slowly and in perfect control. He went down the shaft to a depth of 24m in very bad visibility to a point where he perceived the sump to be complex. Geoff now had to return to base as he did not have sufficient air for a long dive at depth. Cutting the line, he deliberately left the end free, as he suspected that the line had been pulled into tight spots and would perhaps be impossible to follow if tied off at the far end. He surfaced after five minutes underwater.

We then helped Geoff to walk fully kitted to the upstream sump. While I was tying off his line I foolishly put my ammunition box down and while I wasn't looking the NCC stole another one of my Mars Bars.

There was only just room at the sump to comfortably seat the large numbers of cavers who had turned up on this trip. Geoff made another professional departure and we settled down to wait. After about five minutes some of the group announced that they had pressing business to attend to on the surface and set off out. Over the next forty minutes several more people apparently lost interest in the fate of our diver and disappeared without a word. After an hour only Derek, Dave Timmins and myself were left. Another fifteen minutes passed, Geoff was now overdue and we were getting cold and starting to worry. I started to hold on to the end of the line hoping to feel it twitch. We turned out our lights so as to be able to see the first faint glow of our Geoffs' lights as he returned. We started to say things like, "Well, either he has surfaced or he is about to run out of air." I hate waiting for divers to return to base.

We were very relieved when we saw light coming from the bottom of the sump pool. Geoff emerged shortly afterwards and was somewhat surprised by the lack of carriers remaining. He explained to us how he had surfaced after a dive of 80m in an underground lake in a large chamber. A clean washed, walking size streamway wound on for 250m to another sump. He had noticed a low wet inlet and a dry side passage but explored neither to any conclusion. A superb find. We stored about half the gear for future use and set off out carrying very heavy loads. We eventually emerged totally shattered after a twelve-hour trip.

We would have liked to continue our exploration of King Pot the following weekend. Unfortunately heavy rain prevented us from doing so. For several weekends, in fact, we would travel to Ingleton only for it too be wet to go down. Despondency would set in and we would end up spending too much time and money in pubs and discos. Eventually the weather relented a little and we were able to get back to work. The plan was for Geoff and myself to go through the upstream sump while Lugger and Henpot dug in an inlet near to the start of the upstream sump.

The cave was still very wet; in fact, we went down in near flood conditions. I dived first and managed to have an epic. I was carrying an ammunition box containing survey equipment, food and spare lights. I had put some lead weights in the box to reduce the buoyancy. Half way down the shaft the box imploded and flooded; it became very heavy and sent me plummeting to the floor at 11m depth. As a result of my rapid descent I failed to equalise either my ears or sinuses and they hurt rather a lot. At this time I hadn't worked out the reason for my uncontrolled descent and was rather confused. I knew that I had gained all the depth I needed to pass the sump so decided to continue anyway. I made very slow progress due to bad visibility, very high water flow, and the enormously heavy ammo box. On surfacing in the lake at the far end I didn't quite make it out of the water and sank back down to the bottom of the sump. By now I had identified the ammo box as the problem and dragged my way, hand over hand, up the boulder floor of the underwater part of the lake chamber, all the time finning madly. Upon reaching the surface for the second time I managed with a great effort to hurl the ammo box onto dry land. I then was able to get out of the water suffering from a severe headache and painful ears. My mask was half full of blood, but fortunately the bleeding had by now stopped. I was very annoyed with myself for making such a hash of the dive.

Geoff arrived shortly afterwards and I suggested that we have a Mars Bar each out of the ammo box I had carried through the sump with such pain and effort. To our disgust we found that once again the NCC had managed to steal the Mars Bars, even though I had been closely guarding our supplies. They hadn't taken everything though and we made do with half a bar of chocolate each.

The lake chamber and the streamway beyond I found to be very impressive. I helped Geoff to the far upstream sump while enjoying immensely splashing along the fine watercourse. While he dived I set off to explore side passages. First I went up the wet inlet to the left of the sump Geoff was diving. I followed it for about 30m. to a point where the constricted passage ahead of me started to fill up with water. I was effectively damming the stream and in alarm I backed out of the inlet as fast as possible.

Next I looked at a dry passage where a climb out of the streamway led to a small chamber with a passage continuing onwards. After a few metres of crawling I emerged in another chamber. To my astonishment

I could hear voices and sounds of digging! Lugger and Henpot were clearly close at hand!

I announced my arrival at the far end of their dig: "Ahem, excuse me, is this King Pot?" Ecstatic whoops from the diggers and, "Aye up Pooh, make yourself useful and move some of these boulders!"

Soon Lugger and Henpot popped out of the floor of the chamber and rushed off towards the streamway, making a lot of noise as they went.

Meanwhile, Geoff had dived for 35m in a shallow sump. It was wide and low with appallingly bad visibility. He lost the way on despite an exhaustive search. Geoff returned to base and was amazed to see not just one light, but three. He later told me that his first thoughts were that I had finally lost the plot completely and had started ferrying porters through the upstream sump.

I went out through the new sump bypass with Lugger and Henpot and carrying Geoff's boots while Geoff exited through the sump carrying my bottle. We had a huge amount of gear to be taken out of the cave and set off from the base at the first upstream sump with debilitating loads. I was very weary and just switched off and went on to a sort of auto pilot mode, not really thinking much, just keeping going. This worked to a degree, but at one point I was brought back to full awareness by Henpot shouting at me. "Aye up Pooh, why are you crawling along walking size passage, dragging bottle and ammo tin behind you?" I hadn't noticed that for a change this particular bit of cave was not a crawl. At King Henry Hall we were so knackered that we decided to leave most of the gear behind for another day.

With much lighter loads we set off, moving faster. I did have one problem though. My carbide lamp was playing up really badly and kept going out. I couldn't understand why as I had not half an hour earlier fettled it. I moaned about this to Lugger, who showed no sympathy, laughed, and said that he was having no trouble at all with his carbide lamp. I decided that I would just have to give the light another good cleaning and maybe another fill of carbide. I started to work on it. Realisation dawned—it wasn't my light. My good light had been switched for a useless one. How, I could not comprehend.

"Lugger you bastard!!" I shouted at the rapidly departing pair of boots ahead of me.

I didn't return to Australia as planned after three months. In fact I stayed in the UK for more than two years. I did some of my best caving and cave diving during this period, mostly with the NCC and sometimes with Geoff Yeadon or the new generation of ULSA. At first I lived on my savings, then I started doing odd jobs, like working on the Christmas mail. I moved into Dave Brook's house in Leeds 6 and then into a bed-sit in a large house, 229 Hyde Park Road, also in Leeds 6. My neighbours in this house included Ginge Hewson, one of my earliest friends in ULSA and Bernard Newman, aspiring climbing magazine editor. My prize possession apart from the cave diving equipment I had now purchased was a rather ropey colour TV. Bernard would invite some of the top climbers of the day around to watch themselves in climbing films on my TV. He would introduce me to people like John Bancroft with something along the lines of "This is Pooh, he doesn't climb but he's a cave diver and nearly dies every weekend."

Not long after moving in with Ginge and Bernard, I got a job as a technician at Leeds University Mining Department. It was my privilege to work for Dr Jack Myers, co-author of the caving classic, *Underground Adventure*. We would often talk about caving. Jack would always give me time off for cave rescues and his office was often enlivened by caving characters turning up unexpectedly to see him. One day Mike Boon dropped by carrying a cardboard box containing some manky looking bread and cheese. Boon had just returned from some epic in Mexico or the jungle in Guatemala or somewhere!

Geoff Yeadon had dropped out of teaching and was currently homeless, sometimes sleeping in his Morris 1000 and sometimes on various peoples' floors. He would often turn up at my bed-sit, covered in grime after a day working on a building site. With a grin he would announce, "I've decided to go terminal drinking D.W." I would always agree and we would often get ourselves into some very seedy situations in the rougher parts of Leeds.

Derek Crossland lived nearby to me in Leeds 6 and often we drank beer together in the Royal Park during the week. One evening he helped me out greatly by repairing my car. I was very grateful as I didn't have the money to pay a mechanic and I'm hopeless with cars myself. I promised to buy him a lot of beer to repay him. He was surprised and said there was no need for me to do this as I was a mate and he had wanted to help me. He was a very nice bloke.

One time on a trip with the NCC exploring Strike Series in the Kingsdale Master Cave I got annoyed with Derek. He had placed some bang and asked me for the dets. "I haven't got them," I replied. "Yes you have, I put them in your carbide container to keep them dry," Derek informed me. "Are you mad!" I exploded. "You could have blown me up!" Derek really couldn't see my problem and just grinned. I started to go on about how heat could be generated if the carbide got wet and spontaneous ignition and stuff like that. I was having trouble maintaining my indignation though and pretty soon I started laughing. I could never stay annoyed with Derek (or any of the NCC) for long.

During this period the caving world suffered two very sad losses with the deaths of Oliver (Bear) Statham and Ian Plant. These tragic events had, I think, the effect of making me question the life I was leading with its berserk drinking sessions and risky underground adventures. Also, my low wages at Leeds were not sufficient to service debts I had left in Australia as a result of ill advised 'investments.' I realised I was going broke when I had to sell my old Austin Maxi to pay the rent. Thatcher was in power and calling for massive cuts in education. I was under no illusions about my dispensability in the mining department and unemployment was rising. I was without qualifications and thirty years old.

I knew there was big money to be made in oil exploration and resolved to get into this industry. With the help of contacts I had made at the University and, I suspect, a good reference from Jack Myers, I got an interview with an oilfield service company for a position as a mudlogger. The guy who interviewed me did not seem impressed and told me so. I was on the verge of walking out of the interview when he said, "I can tell you know absolutely nothing about geology and we normally hire geology graduates. Still, we have a high turnover of staff as everybody is pissed off and we are expanding rapidly. We may be desperate enough to hire you: but don't count on it." He did hire me and within weeks the company said they were going to transfer me to its Australian operation. I was terrified—I was totally untrained and still wasn't quite sure what my job entailed! My employer had lied to the Australian oil company I was to work for and had described me as "A top hand with two years' experience."

Once I knew I was on my way to Australia again, I told the company that I needed to have a month to move out of my flat and sort out my finances. This was partly true but really I wanted to do just a few more caving trips in the Dales before devoting my energies entirely to the oil business.

Since my initial trips down King Pot I had been down a few more times with the NCC. I had helped them explore some of the very low and flood liable passages named Grasshopper Series which is upstream of the first upstream sump. We were hoping to open up a 'Valley Entrance' and indeed some of Grasshopper Series seemed to come very close to Kingsdale Beck. On one of these trips I had to go into a horrible muddy tube that Lugger had entered in order to rescue him. He was on his way back and he became stuck. I had just arrived on the scene having been off exploring some other dreadful passage. He shouted in alarm that the liquid mud was rising around his face and he was in trouble. I shot in to the tube head first and grabbed hold of his hand and pulled. Out popped Lugger none the worse for wear. His guard was momentarily down due to his fright and he forgot himself so far as to sort of thank me, saying, "Just for once Pooh I was glad to see your ugly face." This didn't last for long though and he soon regained his composure and threw some of the disgusting glutinous mud at me. I like Lugger a lot.

The explorations of the far reaches of King Pot were very worrying and I was always half expecting to be confronted with a wall of water rushing towards me from the beck. It occurred to me that what was needed was the use of Bob Makin's amazing inductaphone equipment. We could then accurately pinpoint the end of Grasshopper Series and also stay in voice contact with the surface, thereby being kept posted as to the weather conditions. Wanting a memorable trip before departing for Australia, I mentioned this possibility to Bob. At first he was not too sure, saying, "I don't like the NCC!" I could understand this; the NCC had quite likely done something despicable to Bob or his club, the Viking Cave Club, at some time in their murky past! I said words to the effect that the NCC were okay once you got to know them. I don't know for sure if this conversation led to Bob agreeing to get involved with the NCC. Anyway, he is a nice bloke and soon a trip was underway.

My job was to crawl to the very end of Grasshopper Series carrying a very compact transmitter that Bob had designed especially for the trip. Prior to this a voice contact with the surface had been established in a slightly larger part of the series. As I lay flat out in the passage, keeping the transmitter in a vertical position as instructed, I reflected that this high tech approach to caving was really catching on. Safe in the knowledge that it was still fine outside, I decided that this was indeed the way to cave. Why be scared stiff all the time? Still, it was a cold, wet, miserable spot and I was glad when a 'runner' came along the passage and said, "Okay Pooh, we have a fix—you can come back now."

As a result of this successful trip the NCC started a dig in the part of the beck closest to the end of Grasshopper Series. In their quirky way, they named the dig 'Wookey Hole.' This did not go though and after a lot of hard work at another site close by they opened up the valley entrance to King Pot. By this time though I was in Australia working on oil rigs, trying hard to build a career and make up for my rather 'misspent youth.' It was to be more than a decade before I returned to these intimidating passages, and under circumstances beyond my wildest imagination back then at the start of the 1980s.

"Hey Pooh, can you take these?" Not even more bottles! I went back into the waist-deep pool and waded to the middle of the duck. Two huge air cylinders (180 cubic feet I think) were passed through to me and I staggered out of the duck backwards and put them down with all the rest of the gear. I could hardly believe that this huge pile of equipment could be worn by just two divers and that they would actually be able to move underwater with it all. There were twelve cylinders, and most of them were very large indeed. As well as the air, there were all the other items of cave diving kit. Fins, lead, a line reel, several lights and many other bits and pieces, including sophisticated dive computers that until now I had only read about.

Glad that it was an easy carry to Kingsdale Master Cave downstream sump, I selected some equipment from the pile and set off into the cave. I moved along the passage on hands and knees, and could hear the resonant sound of bottles clanging on rock, as both ahead and behind me other cavers struggled with their loads.

This was 1991 and five divers were making very rapid progress towards the goal of linking King Pot and the West Kingsdale Master Cave. Geoff Yeadon diving with Geoff Crossley, and John Cordingly diving with Russel Carter were making alternate pushes from KMC towards King Pot. Rupert Skorupka was pushing the downstream King Pot sump. Geoff and Geoff were diving on this occasion. They did not expect to make the connection on this trip, but planned to narrow the gap between the far point reached in downstream King Pot, by Rupert and their finds beyond Cobble Inlet. I had been keen to help out with the carry, as apart from the opportunity of being involved, in a small way, with a totally amazing cave diving project, the majority of the other carriers were from the NCC. I have always enjoyed caving with this wild and unconventional group of individuals.

After several trips carrying gear along the Roof Tunnel, I climbed down the short ladder pitch to the Kingsdale Master Cave in time to help Geoff Yeadon kit up—just as I had done more than a decade earlier, when with Bear he had been preparing to do the first through dive to Keld Head. It was different this time. There was no film crew on this trip. I remembered all the bustle and hype surrounding the through dive and I was glad that on this trip only cavers were involved and we could do the job we had come to do without all the stage management and general farting around of the media.

When the divers were ready to go, I was still astonished at the huge amount of equipment they were carrying. It seemed to me that every part of their bodies had something attached. Hoses of differing sizes seemed to connect it all together. Out of water, they could not move unassisted. I was horrified—they had to go through squeezes! How were they going to do that? How could anybody have the strength required to propel themselves underwater for several kilometres decked out like this? They planned to spend up to an hour and a half decompressing in one place on their return to base. The thought of just staying still in a sump for this length of time for some reason filled me with as much dread as the sheer length and depth of the dive they were undertaking. I realised of course that Geoff and Geoff had been gradually building up to an astonishing level of ability, dive after dive, year after year. They were very likely the best cave divers in the world. Yes, logically I could appreciate that this dive was feasible; emotionally it scared me stiff, and I was very worried about my two friends.

We watched the lights in the sump fade away and disappear, then made our way back to the surface. There was nothing to be gained by waiting around for five hours or more when the entrance was less than half an hour away. We killed the time walking around Kingsdale and were back at the sump at the agreed time. After five and a half hours, the divers returned, tired and jubilant. They had broken through to a large phreatic tunnel at 30m depth and had pushed on for 165m, directly towards King Pot. They named the new passage, 'Sea of Tranquillity.'

Due to work commitments I did not help on any of the other dives, from KMC towards King Pot. When I heard that the connection had been made I resolved to help out when the through dive from King to Keld Head was attempted.

Eight o clock in the morning and I was already hypothermic! Talk about bad management. Steve Redwood was not impressed, as he had taken my advice and, like me, worn dry caving gear, not a wetsuit, down King Pot. I had completely forgotten about the low wet crawls and claustrophobic duck, between the East Kingsdale valley entrance and the King Pot downstream sump. Even though I had been in on the original exploration of these passages, I had somehow remembered them as comfortable hands and knees crawling!

Why such an early start? *The Observer* newspaper had agreed to supply free beer in the Hill Inn, if we could get the dive over and done with in time for the 3 p.m. copy deadline. We had assembled at Braida Garth at around 5 a.m. Once again the NCC and many other cavers had turned up in force to help Geoff and Geoff. Sid Perou had landed the job of filming the event. We carried the once again enormous amount of equipment over to the concealed valley entrance to East Kingsdale. The NCC could get permission from the farmer to open up this 'easy' way in to King Pot for special events like exploratory diving and rescues.

Lugger dug open the entrance and very quickly people and equipment disappeared into the hole. Sid wasn't ready and missed getting any footage of the start of the carry. Steve Redwood and myself were behind Terry Whitaker, whose light failed just as he left daylight. I was not surprised at this, as back in my days with ULSA in the '70s this sort of equipment failure was normal. Terry was an old ULSA member and I remembered with amusement a trip I had done with him to the bottom of the Pierre St. Martin in France, when his light had been most unreliable and he had kept walking into walls. (As it turned out I could hardly criticise Terry for incompetence as on the same trip, I fell 18m down a pitch near the bottom of the cave and had a lot of trouble getting out.)

Back in the present: Terry demanded that I supply him with light from behind, which was a bit hard in a squeeze while carrying a large bottle. Steve, a modern caver, was not used to this sort of thing and was unimpressed when I explained that this was quite all right as Terry was a caving hero from the 1960s. Sid, still on the surface, was by now getting very upset as he felt he was missing all the action. He had wanted us to help him with his filming equipment, but we had left him as we felt we had quite enough stuff to carry already. Indeed Terry was carrying a load of 130 lbs which the NCC had prepared especially for him. It contained mostly lead and also a rock.

Terry, Steve and myself made slow progress towards the downstream sump, and I started to remember just how horrible the lower reaches of King Pot are. Terry could not work out why he was having so much trouble with his load and why he was slower than everybody else. It had been years since I had been through a duck with as little airspace (less than 5 cm) as the duck in the sump bypass. As I weaved my way through it with my helmet off and nose to the roof, I got in a bit of a flap and started to breathe in water. "Bloody Hell," I thought, "I used to push this sort of thing!" Indeed I had been one of the first people through this very duck and literally hadn't noticed it.

As we continued down the main streamway to the downstream sump, people who had delivered their loads to base started to pass us, on their way out of the cave. When we arrived at the sump nearly everybody else had gone on out. Terry, still without a light, attached himself to the small group remaining and they all set off to the surface, leaving Steve and myself waiting for the divers to arrive. We were now very cold and I was deeply regretting wearing 'dry grots.'

After a short wait Geoff and Geoff arrived at base along with Sid and Gavin Newman. Gavin was taking the photos for the *Observer* and had, I think, also become involved in some way with Sid's operation.

Sid still hadn't got any footage and he had only managed to get his filming equipment to the duck, where it had been left behind. He wanted Steve and myself to go back with him through the duck with the loads we had already carried to the sump and then film us carrying this gear back to the sump. I refused to do this. Steve was more willing to help than I and we agreed to go back through the duck to help Sid carry his gear to the dive base, in order to film the divers. He could forget all about re-enactments of the carry!

We had a very nasty time ferrying the filming gear through the duck. I was by now shivering violently due to having been immersed in water several times wearing totally inadequate 'dry grots.' Steve bore it all stoically, in contrast to my constant moaning and groaning. I warned him that if he continued like this he was in danger of ending up as Sid's next assistant. He was showing all the signs and could end up as the next of a long line of unfortunates stretching way back to the 1960s.

At last we got Sid's gear to the sump and we started to film. Almost immediately one of the filming lights failed; but with it's dying glimmers we managed to get a sequence of us pretending to arrive at the sump. At last the divers started to kit up. I helped them do this while the others filmed and took photographs.

Once again I was astonished at the huge amounts of equipment the divers were wearing. I remembered when Geoff last dived in this site, back in 1978. Then he had gone in with two 40 cubic feet bottles. This time he was wearing six large cylinders and was embarking on a dive of more than three kilometres at a maximum depth of 35m. The sump pool was frothy and the water peat stained. Visibility was going to be bad. When the divers were ready they didn't say much—they just checked their gear and set off calmly.

Steve and myself helped Sid and Gavin out with the filming gear. We went and had a look at the Lake Chamber and I amused Steve with my nostalgic account of how I had helped Geoff Yeadon explore this part of the system and how I had never been able to find a way of preventing the NCC from stealing my Mars Bars.

The sun was shining when we reached the surface, and I was glad. It had been a very cold trip, and I was feeling very shaky on my feet and in need of warming. As soon as we were out of the entrance, Lugger started to fill it in and cover it over with large rocks. "What if Geoff and Geoff have to turn back?" I ventured. It was always possible that the lines could be damaged or Cobble Inlet becomes impassable. Lugger didn't consider these things possible and I felt he was almost certainly right. Still, I had a horrible vision of Geoff and Geoff making a desperate return, getting the bends and then being trapped at the entrance. I decided to go back and check after two hours.

After a drive down to Ingleton for a late breakfast, Steve and I were back at the King Pot Valley Entrance. I removed the grass sods and, feeling rather foolish, shouted at the rocks: "Hello anybody there?" No reply. Just to make sure I picked up one of the rocks and banged it down on the metal lid. Still no reply, so we covered over the entrance again and went over to Keld Head where a number of people had already arrived to welcome the divers. Several had brought picnic hampers and cans of beer and a convivial atmosphere was starting to develop.

Four and a half hours after the dive had started, Gavin Newman kitted up and went in to see if there was any sign of the divers. Very soon he was back and reported that they were just a short distance inside, decompressing. We were all ecstatic, and the cans of beer started to disappear rapidly now that the tension of the waiting was over.

Five and a half hours after the start of the dive the divers surfaced and this time we clapped and cheered. Lugger, dressed in normal clothes, waded into the water to help them out. He had his pipe in his mouth and was holding a can of beer. He slipped and in an effort to keep his beer out of the water, fell over completely and put out his pipe. The divers helped him out of the water.

5

Through the Past Darkly

When I was serious about my caving most trips I did were done as part of some sort of longer term project that either I or my friends were involved in. For instance, the exploration of caves in the Three Counties System, or the Black Keld System. Sometimes I would do trips not directly linked to any one project but with some loose sort of connection to one. For instance short dives in Keld Head or Wookey Hole, undertaken for training for an exploration dive in somewhere like Langcliffe. Or perhaps doing long surface shafts on ladders, or later by SRT, as training for a specific foreign expedition. On occasions though I seem to have done some trips quite spontaneously with no planning at all and in no way associated with any perceived 'grand plan.' The random and arbitrary nature of these ventures often resulted in farcical situations and some worrying moments. Please bear with me as I recount some dubious adventures.

Dowber Gill Passage

When I was a schoolboy and had just started caving I took a book out of the public library called *Potholing Beneath the Northern Pennines*, by David Heap. One chapter was devoted to the through trip from Providence Pot to Dow Cave via Dowber Gill Passage. This writing inspired me, as David Heap managed to not just describe the cave, but to get across the excitement of the venture and the beauty of Wharfedale. He took the reader, along with the caving group as they walked through the picturesque village of Kettlewell in winter, and with crisp new snow on the ground. I could imagine their anticipation as they trudged up the hillside, leaving footprints in the snow, to the entrance of Providence Pot, there to disappear underground. I wanted very much to follow in the footsteps of these cavers and a few years later I did.

Late summer in 1970 I was back in Leeds early from the University's long break. Predictably I had failed some of my first year exams and in order to continue as a student at Leeds I had to pass these exams as 're-sits.' I had nowhere to live and was dossing at Tony White's place. (Tony had failed some of his second year exams and he too was back in Leeds early.) He was annoyed at me because I wasn't helping with the rent. I had spent all my money caving in France over the summer and was trying to live on porridge, potatoes and some sort of powdered gunge that was supposed to provide all of the body's nutritional requirements when mixed with water. It tasted dreadful and Tony was wisely guarding his food, should I be tempted to 'borrow some.'

I was concerned that I would be chucked out of my course and have to leave the exciting world of Leeds caving. This motivated me to actually do quite a lot of swotting. One evening though I got overloaded with some particularly hard calculations to do with Quantum Mechanics and I started to read a mountaineering book by Walter Bonatti instead. I was very inspired with this hair-raising account of his solo assent of The Dru —a total epic that made me want to have an exciting solo adventure. I had wanted to do a long solo trip since reading in some caving textbook that one should under no circumstances go caving alone. Besides, my friends had recently been doing it and had been having some pretty mad times. Both Dave Brook and Tony White had gone a few miles into Mossdale, on different days, and alone. Dave had not even bothered to take a spare light or even any carbide to refill his one lamp. Ian Gasson had gone to the end of Langcliffe on his own and actually pushed a tight passage. As for Alf Latham, he had gone down Swarthgill Hole alone and had ended up feeling his way out when his one light, an unreliable Nife Cell, had cratered on him.

I had still not done Dowbergill Passage and it was high on my tick list. I knew that this was considered a fairly hard but not extreme trip and, requiring no ladders or ropes, it would be a nice solo challenge. Quantum Mechanics abandoned, I started to pack my rucksack in readiness for an early departure the following morning. I mentioned to Tony that I was planning to solo Dowbergill. He grinned a bit and said something about me not expecting him to come on the rescue.

It rained a lot in the night but I set off anyway, having convinced myself that the trip would be more sporting if wet and that anyway people didn't seem to drown in Dowbergill, only become trapped for a while. I was a bit hungry but I had the good fortune to find four bananas lying in the road. It was not long after sticking out my thumb that I got a really good lift all the way to Skipton. The trip was going well and Walter Bonatti would no doubt have been most impressed so far!

I arrived in Kettlewell early in the afternoon and started up the hill-side for Providence.

It was raining very heavily by now but I tried not to worry too much about this minor detail. Anyway I was busy conceiving a very cunning plan! ULSA were having difficulty getting permission to go down Langcliffe Pot. We had always walked up to Langcliffe from Scargill. Now if we continued to do this we would very likely be seen and told to leave the area. But what if we were to start the walk in to Langcliffe from Kettlewell and pretend we were doing Dowbergill? Once up on to the limestone benches and out of view we could traverse along the Dale to Langcliffe, undetected. In fact we did later implement this plan with great success until we were daft enough to get trapped by floods in Langcliffe.

I was soaking wet by the time I found Providence entrance. I hurriedly found a place to hide my rucksack and changed into my wetsuit. I had collected together an assortment of dubious torches and other spare lighting including candles and packed these items in a small ex-army haversack, along with the obligatory Mars Bar and one or two tasty tit-bits I was sure Tony would not miss. Also, I carried plenty of spare carbide and some carbide light spares. Was I well equipped or what? With a last look around at the rain-swept fell I set off into the cave.

Once my eyes had adjusted to the gloom of the poorly lit cave I started to make good speed. I found Providence a friendly enough cave. There was some crawling, one or two short squeezes and some nice easy passages where I could walk or at least progress at a stoop. I frequently wandered off route, along side passages, but soon realised I was going the wrong way and retraced my steps. I knew for sure I was on course for Dowbergill Passage when I reached The Palace, a large chamber described briefly in my battered copy of *Pennine Underground*, or *PU* as we called this inadequate and incomplete volume which passed for a guide book back in the early seventies. I confidently strode down this chamber to a small hole in the floor. This I entered and climbed on down into a place called The Dungeon. With ease I descended further down a calcite boss into Depot Chamber. After a short look around I exited right under some excellent formations into a crawl. I could now hear the welcome sound of a large stream. I knew I must be close to Dowbergill Passage now and feeling very pleased with my navigation scampered along the crawl. Very soon I popped out at Stalagmite Corner. I was in Dowbergill—I had it in the bag (or so I thought). I had been mildly worried about finding my way through Providence. I had seen a survey and it had looked a bit complicated. But Dowbergill was shown as a straight line, going straight to Dow Cave. How could I go wrong now? My optimism was confirmed when after setting off down the stream passage and scrambling easily over some boulders I entered a large easy walking passage—a doddle! I ran along this blissfully unaware that I was about to become rather confused for quite a few hours. Here is a quote from *Northern Caves* published sometime after my minor epic in Dowbergill:

The traverse of Dowbergill remains one of the classic caving expeditions in the district. It has also been the scene of many rescues.

The survey plan of a simple straight line belies the intricate and at times exasperating problem of route finding within a twenty metre vertical range in the high rift passages.

Well, really the memory of my fraught journey through the hillside to Dow Cave is somewhat blurred. Here are a few highlights!

This bloody confusing boulder choke with really well-worn incorrect leads to nowhere! And when I did find the way through it was in the first hole I had investigated and dismissed as too tight. Or the really annoying traverse with no apparent handholds or footholds which I fell off. Then there was a definitely exasperating climb up over muddy flowstone which was so slippery I kept sliding back down it. Indeed there were many really 'interesting' intricate route finding problems in the vertical plane of this perfectly straight rift passage. These were all solved in the fullness of time but with only slightly more expertise than the physics problems I had so recently been attempting.

My carbide lamp kept playing up but all of my collection of battery-powered lights was even worse. After regaining the stream after another confusing boulder choke I stripped the carbide lamp down and gave it a good fettling. It started to behave after this and I celebrated with a Mars Bar.

Still I was making progress and going fairly well overall. I was getting a bit concerned though. Once in a while I would find myself back at stream level and every time I did there was more water than the time before. The cave seemed to be flooding. I decided to stay as high as possible in the rift. As I progressed forward I gradually gained height until I had climbed right up to the top of the rift and I could tell from the texture of the passage that few people had been this way. I knew I was off the normal route (again!) but felt I should try to force it through at this level because of the high water below. Thrashing along on my side with my lower shoulder and arm stretched out in front and the other arm trailing behind I made slow progress along the rift. Unfortunately, instead of the passage size increasing as I had hoped it would, it gradually got tighter and tighter until I realised that I would have to reverse back out. I knew this would be very strenuous indeed but at this stage I was merely annoyed, not scared. Then my right foot got jammed in a small keyhole-shaped hole in the floor. I could not move forward or backward. I thrashed around to try to free myself. This was a serious mistake because my carbide light fell off my helmet and down into the rift. I could see it below me in a slot only a few inches wide—out of reach in my present position. Then the flame went out. I told myself not to panic, to lie still and think things through. A logical analysis of my plight was required. I itemised the good and bad points of my situation and came up with something along these lines.

Bad Points:

1. I am badly stuck.

2. It is totally dark.

3. I am off route.

4. I am on my own.

5. I'm feeling exhausted.

6. Come to think of it, since stopping moving I'm feeling rather cold.

7. Six bad points is enough for now. Let's move on to the good points.

Good Points:

1. I've got spare lights.

2. Tony White will call out the rescue team if I do not turn up at his place after a day or two.

3. I can move upwards and downwards for as much as three inches.

4. That seems to be about it for the good points.

5. That seems to be about it for the good points.

More Bad Points:

7a My spare lights are all crap and anyway I can't reach them as they are in this bag which is totally jammed between me and the side of the rift.

Then I had a plan!

I started to move my chest slowly up and down in the tight rift I was trapped in. As I moved upwards I breathed in. As I moved downwards I breathed out. Very slowly the bag containing my spare lights moved upwards. After several rests and what seemed like an hour the bag had moved sufficiently upwards to enable me to shuffle around in the passage and to my delight I was able to wrench my right foot free. I then was able to reverse out of the tight section, pulling the precious bag along at arm's length. Once back to a place I could sit up in I carefully opened the bag and found the least crap torch. I switched it on and it seemed like a searchlight after the total darkness from which I had thankfully emerged. I now had a quick rest and the last of my food. To make myself as manoeuvrable as possible I removed my boots and helmet and re-entered the tight rift to rescue my carbide. To my utter relief I retrieved it after many contortions and just as the torch flickered to final extinction. I reversed backwards out of the rift to where I had left my boots and helmet and in a short while had my carbide light operational.

Well, I had wanted an adventure, and here I was having one. Not quite so hair-raising as some of Walter Bonatti's, but nonetheless a good story for the pub. I realised with pleasure that it was ULSA club night in the 'Swan with Two Necks' in a little over 24 hours' time. I was going to be there for sure.

I started to climb back down towards the stream and at the same time take the best route making progress upstream. I realised that I was probably going to have to stay at or near stream level, flood or not. Pretty soon I was back in the streamway but at least it was still possible to move against the power of the water.

The route finding started to get easier now and I moved along the rift, mostly at stream level. Rather worryingly I could tell that the water level was still rising and sometimes I had to traverse above fast moving deep water. Still this was much more fun than getting lost and stuck and I felt fairly confident that I was getting close to the link with Dow Cave. I started to compose in my mind the tale of this solo journey I would tell my friends in the pub back in Leeds. No need to dwell too much on the more incompetent incidents. I was sure that even Walter Bonatti would have edited the stories of his epics a little.

All this fantasising came to an abrupt halt when I entered a sort of a chamber, really just an enlargement of the rift. Ahead of me was a near vertical wall below which the inky black water of Dowber Gill emerged from a rather definite, no nonsense sort of sump!

It was a long way back to Providence Pot and I was tired. I simply could not accept the idea of having to go back. I had a quick look around for a bypass of some sort but I was almost sure there would be none. This was just procrastination really, side passages not being much of a feature in Dowber Gill. I had a look at the rock wall above the sump. I felt it could perhaps be climbed; also, the sump pool would make falling off slightly less unacceptable. So I set off tentatively upwards. About 3 metres up I found a small slot going in the direction of the upstream rift. Unfortunately, it was far too tight and a very strong wind was screeching out of it. Depressingly this indicated to me that this was most likely the only above-water continuation of the rift. I carried on anyway, the climbing getting harder and harder, until I was in a position 4.5 metres above the sump, not being able to go up and not able to reverse my last move. I lingered for a while getting increasingly scared. Just as I felt I could hang on no longer I plucked up the courage to jump clear of the rock. To my utter relief I made a great landing in the sump pool, making a most satisfying splash.

Charged with adrenaline I took several deep breaths and dived into the sump. I don't think it was very long and I emerged on the upstream side in total darkness (carbide lamps are crap in sumps) with the sound of a large underground river roaring in my ears. Also I could feel spray upon my face from a very proper draught. I staggered along a walking size passage in the dark until I felt I was mostly out of the water. With difficulty I ignited my carbide and set off in the spray and wind towards the roar.

Very soon I connected with Dow Cave. It was scary to see a fast flowing river charging towards me from the right and disappearing to the left into a bedding cave with only about 30 cm of airspace. It was draughting though so I knew that the airspace should, in theory, continue to the world outside that I now so wanted to re-enter. Theory and reality are not always the same but I liked this theory and jumped into the torrent. Swept along in the flood all I had to do was to try to navigate through the best looking route by flapping my limbs. I was actually out of control but very soon I saw daylight. Just in time I saw I was about to be washed over a waterfall. I grabbed hold of a branch of a tree and my momentum swung me out of the cataract and neatly onto the path up to the entrance of Dow Cave. I was out! Just as well too as it was raining torrentially.

When I arrived back in Kettlewell it was dark and I was too tired to want to hitch back to Leeds. I camped in a field in my very small plastic tent that I had picked up for £1.50. It was a very low tent and very hard for farmers to see. This was useful and I used it often when hitch hiking. That summer, in France, I had camped in a field and I had been awakened by the sound of heavy machinery. I had looked out of the 'door' and to my horror saw a combine harvester heading straight towards me. I leapt out and waved my arms frantically. The huge machine had ground to a halt and a most irate operator climbed down from his cab and started shouting at me and waving his arms about. I tried to explain in broken French that I was a Speleologist on my way to explore 'Grande Grottes,' no less! His mood changed and he started to laugh. Not quite the reaction I was after but a great improvement from ranting. I was only wearing underpants and perhaps this in some small way affected my credibility. Any way he let me off without calling the gendarme.

This most recent doss ended less embarrassingly, but it was not a good doss. At about 5 a.m. the field flooded. Still, this meant I got off to an early start and ensured my presence at the 'Swan with Two Necks' that evening.

Most of the Happy Wanderers were at the pub as well as many of the older postgraduate ULSA cavers. Many of the younger members were still away on the long summer break. The Wanderers had made yet another discovery somewhere in the Dales and plans were afoot for an ULSA trip to Ireland within the next few weeks. These were exciting times to be a caver in Leeds.

My account of my solo adventure through Dowber Gill in flood drew a mixed response. Dave Brook just laughed and told me that if I wanted to actually do something useful then I could join him and others down Langcliffe that weekend, deladdering and helping him finish off the survey. In fact, if I wanted to go to Ireland I had better be there as the ladders from Langcliffe were needed for the trip. As always I was only too pleased to go caving with D.B. and readily agreed, even though I was still rather sore from my contortions in Dowber Gill.

I told some of the Wanderers about my Dowber Gill adventure and most of them seemed to be only concerned for my future (or lack of it!) and not all that impressed.

Jake said, "Well, young Pooh, God must really be on your side."

Tiny said, "Please don't die—it would be very sad; we like you really."

Ginge (Eric Hewson) said something I couldn't understand about an inflated ego.

Dives in Alum Pot

(or how a cave diver of yesteryear made a comeback by mistake). from *ULSA Review* 15 August 1979, by the author.

One night in a pub I blurted out that I wanted to dive the Alum Pot sump. I wouldn't normally have made such a rash statement but felt safe in the knowledge that everybody considered Alum a useless site and so wouldn't feel like supporting such a foolish venture. Therefore, it was a bit disconcerting when I heard people volunteering to carry for me as this meant that I actually had to do the dive instead of hanging round in pubs in the Dales and Mendips complaining about the lack of enterprise in the younger generation of cavers.

On October 11th 1978, a party consisting of Pauline Barber, Helen Sergeant, Martin Leonard and myself descended Alum under very wet conditions. On reaching the sump, I decided that it was almost undiveable in such circumstances so I only put on one bottle and the minimum of gear to have a quick look round the sump (I was hoping it would either choke immediately or that I could use the obviously heavy current as an excuse for turning back). Unfortunately, the sump was decidedly roomy six metres in, and I couldn't really claim that the current was at all dangerous so I came out, put on twin 50 cu ft bottles and full gear and made as dramatic a re-entry as possible. Fifteen metres in, I reached a rift which seemed too tight so I made a rapid exit feeling that honour had been satisfied. However, Martin didn't believe that the rift was too tight and, after much persuasion, I reluctantly made a second re-entry into the froth-covered sump. This time I managed to pass the rift at a depth of about six metres by going through sideways. Realising I had passed John Southworth's previous limit, I now became quite enthusiastic, especially as the passage seemed to be rising. At 35m from base I lost the way on at a depth of 3m. The visibility was less than one metre and I decided that even Martin would be satisfied with this attempt so I returned, reeling in my line as I went as I had no faith in it passing along a navigable route. It didn't, but after a few minutes I made it back to base.

The following Wednesday saw Simon Garvey, Stuart Herbage, Martin Leonard and myself back at the sump, ready for round two. The cave was just as wet as before but, as I had already tried that excuse, I started to kit up hoping for some sort of inspiration before having to commit myself. Unfortunately, no '0 rings' blew, neither valve leaked and even my ears, always a good stand-by excuse, decided to clear perfectly.

At 35m into the sump I swam around for a while and found the way on. At 40m from base, I reached the top of a black hole stretching away beneath me. This was a bit serious so, remembering my '20 ft shaft' in the upstream Gavel sump, I tied a weight onto a piece of diving line and lowered it into the hole. It touched bottom at about 12m depth and, after reorganising my line, I set off downwards. At the bottom I found a large passage heading gradually down which I fumbled along through the murky water until I was about 46m from base and at a depth of 15m below sump level. The passage continued on downwards and, feeling happy about having opened up another major diving site and unhappy about the route my line was probably following through this complex sump, I tied off and set off towards base, reeling out my line. It soon became apparent that there was no way I could follow my line as it had pulled in to several tight bedding planes and rifts. At one point I met the original line and, as I didn't see it because of the bad visibility, became entangled in it. As I took out my knife to start cutting, I forced myself to remember that many cave diving accidents occur as the result of line difficulties. After about five hectic minutes of cutting, tying and bubble blowing I had the situation vaguely under control and so groped my way out of the Sump.

I really must go back to Alum sump soon as it is, as they say, "full of potential." The possibilities of further progress are high now, especially as I think I've used up most of the available excuses for making an honourable retreat.

Martin certainly brought out the best in me down Alum. We never did go back. Shortly after this trip he got a job overseas and we lost touch.

'Fast forward' to the Jockey Pub, Singapore 1982: I'm trying to find my boss, Dave, who is the manager of our oil field operations in SE Asia. An important fax concerning a new contract has just arrived at the office and I am anxious to bring it to his attention. He had left the office for a wet lunch and it was now four in the afternoon. My worst fears are confirmed: I spot Dave and he is getting well stuck in at the bar.

I attract his attention: "Dave, Pertimina want you to contact them as soon as possible."

"Tell them to get stuffed," he replies.

"Er, I don't think that would help our position in Indonesia much," I venture.

"Have a beer, dear boy—I'll call them tomorrow."

Dave was easily the best boss I had ever had! Several drinks later he heads off home and I turn to leave as well; as there is nobody interesting left in the bar. On the way out to my utter astonishment I almost bump into Martin Leonard.

"What on earth are you doing in here?" I gasp.

"Never mind what I'm doing here, aren't you supposed to be down some cave or something?"

"No, I've given all that up. I'm in the oil business. I'm in Geodata."

Martin looks shocked. "But you have no qualifications and you're always pissed. How did you do it?"

"Oh, bullshit mainly; they didn't believe it but they were desperate."

It turns out that Martin is doing exactly the same job as me, but with one of my employer's competitors. We left the Jockey Pub at closing time. I had tried to get him to 'defect' to my company but he would have none of it.

Caving Pathetically on Mendip

Shortly after my Alum Dives I decided it was time to earn some money as I was rather low on funds. I had been trying to get a job in oil exploration but had been rejected on the fairly reasonable grounds of having no qualifications or relevant experience. Perhaps it would be possible to make some money out of caving? After some thought I came up with a scheme. I would survey Swildon's Hole on the Mendips. Then I would publish it and sell copies at a profit. I reasoned that the only available survey of Swildon's was out of date and as this was such a popular cave, then my survey would sell very well. I needed an assistant for this project and started to scout around for somebody suitable.

To my delight Geoff Yeadon agreed to come along. I stressed to Geoff that this was a serious business venture. I further explained that I had calculated that if we went down Swildon's two days out of three and averaged ten-hour trips, then we could expect to have the survey completed in two weeks. Of course we would have to make sure that we stayed out of the pub as drinking would result in a loss of motivation and seriously jeopardise the project. Geoff agreed to all this and made a suggestion. "There is a need for secrecy here, D.W.," he said with a perfectly straight face. "Why don't we code name this excellent plan of yours 'The Bildon's Mole Project?'"

Why not indeed? We slipped away from the Dales and headed south. We stopped off at Buxton and purchased a compass and clinometer from Caving Supplies. This cost me £55.00 so my scheme was already running at a substantial loss. I told myself that this was actually a very sound investment. We later heard that our appearance in Caving Supplies had started several rumours in the Derbyshire caving world.

When we arrived on Mendip we immediately set off down Swildon's. I had decided that this first trip should be a long one in order to make a good start. I reckoned that we should survey Black Hole Series, Saint Pauls and as much of the survey as we could all in one go.

We made rapid progress to the end of Black Hole and started to survey out. It all went rather slowly and I started to remember that there are quite a few rather unpleasant side passages in Swildon's and all these would have to be included in the survey. We had surveyed about half of Black Hole Series when I noticed a side passage, about the third one already. I pretended not to notice it and carried on down the main route. Geoff was not letting me get away with this.

"D.W. Yeandle, get up that passage immediately!"

"I'm sorry Geoff? What side passage are you talking about?" I replied dishonestly.

Laughter. "You know as well as I do, get along it at once!"

Groans, as I disappear along a squalid tube.

After a while we emerge from the side passage. My wetsuit is in shreds; I'm bruised, muddy, cold and rather pissed off. I'm having second thoughts about *The Bildon's Mole Project*. I really don't want to continue but don't want to admit this to Geoff.

"I'm really enjoying this Geoff," I lie. "How about you?"

"Never been so happy, D.W. old chap."

"I think this is going to take us longer than I thought," I venture.

"As long as you are happy to continue, I will not let you down."

Typical! "Geoff I don't want to do this!"

More laughter. "Thank goodness for that," said Geoff jovially. "I expected you to give up this mad plan long before this! I was wondering how much more I had to put up with."

We headed rapidly out of the cave. 'Bildon's Mole' was over.

So there we were on Mendip; neither of us had a job and we had no real plans for the future. For several days we hung around Mendip, spending rather too much time in the Hunters' Lodge. After a conversation with Martin Grass we regained some sort of direction. Martin, along with Martin Bishop, was diving the coming Saturday in Wookey Hole. "Would we like to join them?" Good idea. I also suggested that Geoff and myself survey Wookey 20. It had not been surveyed accurately and I felt I should at least put my new surveying equipment to some good use.

We had an enjoyable dive to 20 in superb visibility; the only slight mishap being a large slab being dislodged when one of the divers was climbing out of the sump pool in Wookey 20. This unfortunately resulted in the last section of the shallow route line being buried. After a quick look around the two Martins set off out, leaving Geoff and myself to do our survey. It all went rather smoothly with only one small argument temporarily spoiling the proceedings. This occurred when Geoff insisted that I grovel into some disgusting passage in order that the survey be complete.

"This passage is horribly tight and half full of muddy water," I protested.

"D.W., don't be such a poof! You have recently navigated 500 feet of underwater passage! I'm quite sure you can manage this."

Geoff as usual was right and, muttering, I entered the offending passage.

Once we had finished our survey we set off back out through the sump. It was by now evening and the show cave was closed. This was not a problem until we had exited the cave and found ourselves confronted with a large metal gate, with spikes on the top, barring our exit from the show cave grounds. I climbed up to the top of the gate and while precariously perched, Geoff started to pass diving gear up to me. This operation was interrupted by the arrival of the manager of Wookey Hole Caves.

Suspecting burglars, he shone a torch at me and demanded an explanation.

I started to try to explain but fortunately the gentleman now recognised Geoff from a TV film that had been made at Wookey. He was now very friendly and kindly opened the gate for us after I had climbed down.

We then attended a very enjoyable bad taste party at the Priddy Village Hall. Martin Bishop turned up wearing only a jock strap. Phil Collett turned up as me. One lady dressed in tight black leather and brandishing a whip, insisted on chasing Geoff and myself around the dance floor. A Rolling Stones record was being played loudly (*Sympathy for the Devil*) and when Geoff wasn't jumping out of the way of the whip he did his rather realistic Mick Jagger impersonation.

The next day we went back to Yorkshire. Geoff started work on the Keld Head film, *The Underground Eiger.* I continued to look for a means to make some money.

Christmas week 1978: I'm back on Mendip for the festive season and decide to do a pushing dive in Swildon's sump 12. What follows is an extract from Martin Grass's log book.

> *Swildon's Hole 30. 12. 78   Self and Dave Yeandle*
> *Aim: Yeandle to dive sump twelve with 40 cu. ft. bottle and 150 ft. of line reel. I was to be support diver.*
>
> *After spending four hours trying to find sherpas, two lads from the M.E.G. gave us a hand to take gear down to sump two via the Wet Way. The water was high and very cold. At this point Dave decided not to do a pushing trip and to leave some of the gear, fins, line reel etc. Then his main bulb blew so he continued on Aqua -Flashes. We dived sumps two and three and continued to my first dive of sump four, which was a lot easier than I had thought. Once through we met two lads on their way back from free diving to sump nine. When we reached sump five we could not find the airspace (water level rather high). Dave following the line but it led to an underwater mud bank. At this point my light started fading so we decided to abandon the trip and make our way out on two Aqua—Flashes. When we reached sump one the two lads who had gone to nine plus some friends helped get our gear out.*
>
> *When we were at last out there was a hailing snow blizzard and everything iced up (hair, ladder etc.). A pleasant but frustrating trip to sump five.*

Puits Pooh

During the summer of 1972 I spent several weeks caving in the Pierre St Martin in France. At the time it was the deepest cave in the world. Our expedition planned to make it even deeper. One day Dave Gill, Paul Everett and I were pottering around near the bottom of a series of shafts called the Maria Dolores. These shafts were completely separate from the Puits Parment series of shafts which led to the deepest point in the cave. Our plan was to push the bottom of the Maria Dolores to below the depth of the Parment and become 'the deepest men in the world.' On an earlier trip Dave had found a pitch in amongst some nasty boulders at the bottom of a 35m pitch called Puits Sauron. On that occasion he did not have sufficient ladders to explore further. As Dave now prepared to descend the new pitch I decided to have a look around the boulder choke. I found that I could do a tricky traverse over the new pitch and reach a continuing rift. My carbide light was very dim by now so I stopped to fettle it. To my mild surprise I soon had a lovely bright light and could appreciate the nastiness and exposure of the traverse I had just done. I was glad I had had such a poor light earlier as I seriously doubted whether I would have made it into this continuation had I appreciated what I was actually doing. Still, new cave beckoned so I set off to explore. After a few metres I reached another pitch.

I set off back to Dave, quaking a lot this time on the traverse. By now Dave had laddered his pitch and set off down. I quickly followed and we explored several short, sporting wet pitches to a rift that became too tight. Still keen for more exploration we rushed back up the pitches and over the traverse to the new pitch. We hung a ladder down and I set off. At first it was tight and I thrashed around to make downward progress. Soon though the rift widened and I excitedly zipped down the ladder for 20m to a fair sized downward sloping passage. The walls of the cave were clean white limestone and decorated with pretty cave flowers and calcite crystals. I was very pleased with myself and scampered off downwards. Soon I came to another pitch but I had run out of ladder and that was it for the day. This was great, a wide-open cave that was obviously going to go deep. The icing on the cake for me was that we would not have to carry all the ladders back out as we would clearly be returning. Unencumbered, we could make a rapid exit to our wonderful little world of campsite, sun and cheap wine.

Back at Saint Engrace word soon got around that we had broken through in the Maria Dolores. Soon a group of most of the cavers in our rag-tag expedition were gathered around to hear our tale. I felt really chuffed for amongst this group were some of my caving heroes—Dave Brook, Mike Boon and Mike Wooding. I gave a dashing account of our explorations and announced that the world depth record was going to be ours. This produced a round of cheers.

"Hooray! Well done Pooh," exclaimed Mike Boon.

"We'll call the new pitch Puits Pooh," announced Dave Gill.

"Good old Pooh, Puits Pooh!" the whole group shouted.

All a bit over the top really but that was how we used to carry on and we were happy enough! Guess what, we didn't actually break the world depth record. In fact, it all went a bit pear shaped and ended in epics on dangerous, but not deep enough pitches and silly grovellings in passages that refused to go. At one stage Boon ended up lowering me over the edge of a 30m pitch on a rope because we both thought that we were only above a short drop. This caused me great alarm and it took a while to sort the problem out. Boon thought it hilarious.

It was a good expedition though and we had many caving adventures, found quite a lot of new passage and kept getting very drunk and falling over in the field in St Engrace. Apart from that there is a little bit of France that will forever be Puits Pooh.

Caving in the Raw (early 1990s)

Things were not going according to plan. The night before, in the Hill Inn, it had seemed like a great idea to offer my services as a bottle carrier on Alan Downton's proposed Hammer Pot dive. Now I was regretting my involvement as outside the Bradford Pothole Club hut, at Brackenbottom, Alan and myself desperately tried to motivate a motley collection of hung over-cavers. When they had tried most possible excuses, all of which we rejected, they simply drove off with a vague story about doing Simpson's Pot instead.

It was a beautiful summer's day in the Dales. The sun was shining, the birds were singing and a very gentle breeze was rippling through the abundant flowers and trees. Why go caving?—and I very nearly didn't! Alan still wanted to do something though and mentioned that the NCC were doing Strans Gill Pot, with Rupert Skorupka diving a sump. They had already set off but we could follow them down, see the Passage of Time and help detackle. "Okay, let's do it," and we set off.

After driving a while it became clear that we weren't at all sure where Strans Gill was. I thought it was in Littondale while Alan assured me it was in Langstrothdale. He had been to the entrance several years ago, but couldn't quite remember the way. So we drove to Langstrothdale looking for the NCC or their cars. With no sign of either we asked a farmer for permission to visit Strans Gill. "Well, it's not on my land, is it!"—but he told us whose land it was on "and could you get off my land now?"

After some fairly aimless wandering around the right farmer's land we found a streambed that seemed familiar to Alan. Following it upward gave us some enjoyable climbing at around severe standard. This turned out to be an unnecessarily hard approach when we intersected a footpath along which a family with young children was walking. We followed this path and to our surprise found the entrance.

We quickly changed and I set off down the entrance pitch. After a short distance (actually my head was still above ground), I came to an abrupt halt. This was a tight entrance. I climbed back out and tried entering in a different position. I still couldn't get in and tried several more times before deciding that the entrance was too tight for me. What an excellent excuse! Anyway I was probably getting a bit old for this sort of thing. Time for the pub! Why then did I find myself taking off my wetsuit jacket and having another try? In any case I was soon fully underground and committed. The rest of the entrance pitch was slightly less desperately tight and at the bottom I was able to put my jacket back on.

Alan started down the entrance pitch with none of the traumas I had experienced while I carried on into the cave. It was still tight and I was totally appalled when after about 5 metres I encountered an absurdly tight squeeze leading directly to a pitch. I took the wetsuit jacket off again with difficulty and descended the pitch after a struggle. "What a silly carry on," I thought. "Never mind, that must have been the tightest bit."

At the bottom of the pitch (inappropriately named Hope Pitch) I once again put my jacket back on while Alan came on down, again with no trouble whatsoever. The cave really did appear to be getting bigger as I moved forward and I started to enjoy myself. My illusions were shattered when I found myself jammed in an upward squeeze ending in an insanely small hole through which I could see a descending, slightly larger tube. I didn't really want to accept that this was the way on so I reversed out and had a chat with Alan. He managed to convince me that this was indeed the way on, that I was doing very well and he was enjoying caving with me. Reassured, I yet again started to peel off my wetsuit jacket; feeling now a little bit like a tart in a French brothel on a busy Bastille Day. I set off into the tight upward passage pushing my jacket in front of me. My progress was okay but the jacket jammed in the tiny hole. Annoyed, I punched it hard. It shot through the hole and I followed, having to exhale almost totally. The downhill section of the squeeze was bearable and I was pleased to see that my jacket had already carried on down the next pitch. Trouble was, when I reached the pitch, there was no rope going down it and the way on was around to the left.

It turned out to be a short distance to the top of the big pitch of 50 metres. I decided that the pitch descended by my jacket must connect with the main shaft. I felt confident that I would catch up with my jacket at the bottom of the pitch or at worst find it waiting on a ledge.

The pitch turned out to be a moderately wet, spacious rift. I swung around a bit, keeping a lookout for my jacket. I touched down after a superb abseil in high spirits, only to suffer a complete attitude collapse upon finding no sign of my wetsuit jacket. I had lost it!

All through my years of caving this sort of thing has happened and as I waited, now shivering, for Alan to descend, my mind went back over some of these incidents. Like the fin that fell off in Tatham Wife sump or the numerous line reels dumped in haste prior to speedy exits from various sumps. Or the complete set of diving gear, mostly borrowed, abandoned in Langcliffe after a major flood delayed our exit. The more I remembered the worse I felt. Why, only a few weeks previously I had dropped a battery for a Bosch drill into an impenetrable rift in Long Kin West. As a result the trip had been a total waste of time for five people with no progress made at the dig more than 150 metres in depth below the surface.

By the time Alan reached the bottom of the pitch, which is called Charity Pitch (again, in my opinion inappropriately!) I could hear voices ahead. The NCC were on their way out. The lads were surprised and pleased to see us as we strode along the impressive streamway towards them. They found my state of undress very amusing. "I can see your gear hasn't improved," said Lugger. Rupert had a desperate dive in tight sump and it was clear that the lads wanted to get out as soon as possible. It was agreed that Alan and myself carry on down to the Passage of Time and then follow the others out, de-rigging as we went.

We now found the cave to be easy and impressive and soon reached the Passage of Time—a large, dry, wonderfully decorated passage. We followed it until it became low and turned back.

We found ourselves to be an effective de-rigging team and quickly reached the top of the big pitch. Things continued smoothly until the squeeze where I had lost my jacket. I simply could not get through, even with near total exhalation. I reversed back and undressed some more. Wearing only underpants, kneepads and boots and feeling rather foolish I launched myself into the squeeze. I made it and we got the tackle through the obstacle. I was, by now, getting rather cold but reasoned that I might as well leave my trousers off for the rest of the trip. I had had enough dressing and undressing for one day. I did however put my helmet and light back on. Alan now decided to remove his wetsuit jacket as he too was having more trouble going out than in. We seemed to have lots to carry, what with ropes, ladders, SRT gear and articles of clothing.

In what seemed a short space of time we reached the bottom of the entrance pitch. On looking up I was shocked and thought, "How did I ever get down that?" It looked impossible. One metre up I found I couldn't bend my knees sufficiently to make upward progress. This I solved by removing my kneepads. The middle section was impossible with helmet and light and I removed these as well. I was now left wearing underpants and boots. Nothing else!

I knew now that I would make it out but I did have one fear. The NCC could well be lurking near the entrance ready to mount some kind of attack. In the past they have put slugs in my helmet, stolen my Mars Bars, pushed me into a sump (without bottles) and thrown rocks at me.

Pushing my head back into the world, wondering what life was going to be like without the nipple I felt sure had just torn off; I looked nervously around. No NCC! They had gone. I soon found out why when hordes of midges descended upon me. As I leapt for my surface clothing, madly hitting myself in an attempt to be rid of the pests feasting on blood from hundreds of small cuts.

I reflected that some days really don't run according to plan.

0-595-22466-0

Printed in the United Kingdom
by Lightning Source UK Ltd.
9604400001B